Simply More

Simply More

A Book for Anyone Who Has Been
Told They're Too Much

Cynthia Erivo

MACMILLAN

First published in the US 2025 by Flatiron Books
an imprint of Macmillan Books

First published in the UK 2025 by Macmillan
an imprint of Pan Macmillan
The Smithson, 6 Briset Street, London EC1M 5NR
EU representative: Macmillan Publishers Ireland Ltd, 1st Floor,
The Liffey Trust Centre, 117–126 Sheriff Street Upper,
Dublin 1 D01 YC43
Associated companies throughout the world

ISBN 978-1-0350-8601-6 HB
ISBN 978-1-0350-8602-3 TPB

1 3 5 7 9 8 6 4 2

A CIP catalogue record for this book is available from the British Library.

Designed by Leah Carlson-Stanisic

Printed and bound in the UK using 100% Renewable Electricity by CPI Group (UK) Ltd

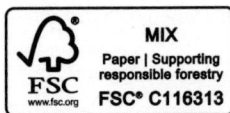

MIX
Paper | Supporting
responsible forestry
FSC
www.fsc.org
FSC® C116313

Visit **www.panmacmillan.com** to read more about
all our books and to buy them.

I want to dedicate this book to:

*Stephanie, a fearless traveler who hasn't even begun
to see how fiercely brilliant she is. I see it.*

*To the one I love: You see me, and you ask me to
expand every day and I am grateful for it.*

*To my mother, the original lioness who has always
believed I could be whatever I want to be.*

*To every single being trying their hardest to
discover who they are, whilst existing in circumstances
that don't allow for them to feel safe or supported;
you have my deepest admiration.*

I am what I am
And what I am needs no excuses

—"I Am What I Am," performed by

Gloria Gaynor

(written by Jerry Herman)

Contents

Part One

Run the First Ten Miles with Your Head

CONTENTS

Part Two

Run the Second Ten Miles with Your Legs

Part Three

Let Your Heart Carry You the Rest of the Way

CONTENTS

Simply More

Dear Reader,

I'm writing this as I prepare for a production of *Jesus Christ Superstar* to be presented at the Hollywood Bowl in which I will play the role of Jesus, a choice that's generated some degree of controversy. This dispute just points out to me, yet again, that sometimes I'm simply more than many people expect or want.

Maybe you're the same?

We who are just a bit more than others are comfortable with often having to navigate the beliefs of those about us—beliefs people hold because of their own biases, beliefs they use at times to keep us contained and insignificant. This is true for members of just about every marginalized group, as well as for those of us who are willing to be deeply, wholeheartedly, and authentically ourselves. We're often monitored and patrolled, told to remain small and unobtrusive lest our freedom affect and inspire others. In order to be fully ourselves, we have to release ourselves from the fear of their judgments and ask ourselves, *What do I really believe?*

And then, we follow that.

But it's a process of becoming and it's taken me years and all kinds of experiences, some glorious, many painful, to get here. I'm sure the same is true for you too.

I've come to believe passionately in the power of singing and performing. For me, these are deeply sacred acts. It isn't simply that I open my mouth and sound comes out. It is not just a frivolous indulgence. Singing only makes sense when you know what it is you are trying to communicate, what or whose story you are trying to tell; maybe what you want to share might be a little profound. Performing is not just about me; it's for my listeners. It's for the person watching who maybe needs that song tonight. It's an offering, a spiritual connection, a gift.

Each of us has our own gifts to give, our own offerings that the world and the people around us hunger for. They are waiting for us to share, for us to make a connection. Though it's hard, we cannot let other people's judgments keep us from giving what we're on this earth to give. I believe that when we don't use our gifts, they fade, so using them to the best of our abilities often means allowing ourselves to be simply more than what others expect.

Yes, I know that is challenging, and I didn't know how to do it at the beginning. But this is a book about how I have come to own myself during those challenging times.

To be faced with people who themselves do not want to be more feels like conflict. Those who are afraid to approach the fullness of their own humanity are often threatened by those of us who are not. We can't let that stop us.

This is exactly what we're called to do, every one of us:

To be the fullest version of ourselves, even when doing so is hard. So even when people try to shout us down. Even when we're ridiculed for being who we are. We're called to keep expanding and growing and evolving. To be more, simply more, of who we really are.

And then, to shed our light on the path of those behind us who are struggling to do the same.

> Yours in love and spirit,
> *Cynthia Erivo*
>
> JUNE 2025

3

Part One

———

Run the First Ten Miles
with Your Head

You Can Run Marathons

I love to run. I really do.

It might be surprising that I'd start a book by declaring my love for anything but music or performing—but I ask that you bear with me. I promise it will make sense once we get there.

So, yes. I love to run. I love the feel of the air on my skin, the pounding of my heart in my chest, the strength of my legs as they propel me forward. I love the feeling of sweat as it gathers on different parts of my body and the cool sensation as it breaks away and slides down my rib cage. I love the work that always precedes the reward, the endorphin high that comes with the miles.

I love going farther than I thought I could, doing what I sometimes worry I won't be able to do. Surprising myself each time I have doubts, and then surprising myself again when I overcome them.

How did I start? The way any of us starts anything: I saw a sign. (Quite literally.)

One day, while in the park, I saw a notice announcing an upcoming 5K for cancer research. I wanted to do something, to contribute. *Why not sign up?* I thought. It was for a good cause.

Almost as soon as that thought appeared in my head, another came through: *I'm not going to be able to do that. I have never even run a 5K.*

Still, I wanted to try. I chose to listen to the first voice because it was the purest and most immediate. It was instinct; it was desire. So, I figured it out. I found a route and I started to run. And I haven't stopped since.

(That is perhaps one of the most important lessons I've learned: Our deepest desires lead us where we want to go. Where we are meant to be.)

In the years since, running has become a meditation. A way of processing. It helps me think, to mull over parts of my daily life, to enjoy silence and feel connected to myself through the sound of my own breath and the movements of my mind. Like a lot of the other things I do, I run because it gives me joy and makes me feel at peace. I have run two official full marathons and four or five half marathons. In training, I log fifteen to twenty-five miles per week. Truthfully, my feet are always in a state of mending. Sometimes,

I take it too far and end up with an injury. When I pass that threshold, I pay for it. I am still learning how much is enough, how balance is important.

I often don't listen to music, books, or podcasts when I run. I was once told by an amazing osteopath, Fabi, that when you run you should be listening to your body, and, for me, he was right. I want my only frequency to be dialed in to my body and what it needs. I listen to my physical self and the deep wisdom and insight it provides as I take each step: What feels strong? What needs support? What feels better than it did last time? How much farther, this time, have I gone? It encourages me to push the finish line farther and challenge myself. It also helps me notice the world around me. It reminds me that I am always evolving, always growing, and that that growth is worthy of reflection and celebration. As humans, no matter where we are in life, we're all changing, all the time, minute to minute, discovering and rediscovering who we are. We are constantly in a wonderful, dynamic state of *becoming*. Running echoes that process. It requires change—in breath, in pace, in direction. When a turn shows up, we take it. When there's a hill, we climb it, and then we feel the ease of the descent and the expanse that appears in front of us. It's control, and it's surrender. Control and surrender.

There are days when I cannot wait to get out and run. But there also are days when I don't want to go outside or even on the treadmill. Those are the days that teach me the most. Those are the days where I have to ask myself, *How can I move past a moment of not wanting to do it? What do I need to feel that desire again?* I sit with that feeling and then figure out what it is I can do that will get me out that door.

The funny thing is this: On those days when I've been able to overcome my own resistance, the run that follows is often absolutely the best.

A few years ago, I wrote a letter to my younger self for a magazine.

Dear Cynthia,

You can run marathons.
In your life and in your work; through the city of New York,
on the stage, and onscreen.
It may not feel like it right now, but your spirit and body are
ready.
There's nothing holding you back.
You might think you aren't far enough yet, but that ache
means you're getting closer.
Please don't stop. You are so close.

Someday soon, you will be where I am right now.
You'll think, "How on earth is this possible? How did this all
happen?"
It will happen because of the work you're doing now
The decisions you are making (both good and bad),
The people you choose to let in.

Don't be afraid of those moments where the world feels
  like it's falling out from under you.
It will happen.
And when it does, don't run.
Let it fall.
When the wreckage comes to rest, you'll be on new sturdy
  ground.

The bigger the dream, the bigger the steps needed to
  achieve it.
Everything is possible.

When you do accomplish a goal, embrace the moment.
Live in it.
Revel in it. The big and the small.
Don't get wrapped up in "what's next?"
A lot of your "nows" are pretty spectacular.
If you don't stop to enjoy them
You'll miss them.

Remember to love and honor the people who come into your
  life and care for you.
When you ask for help, they will be there.
Send them light in your waking moments and when
  you sleep
Wish them warmth, happiness, and safety.
No one can do what we do alone.
Don't try.

You will meet people from all walks of life.
Become a safe space for them to share their stories.
These are the moments of why you're really here.
You are a space where people can see themselves in you.
Make sure whatever is reflected back is bright, sparkly, and
    full of joy and love.

What you give out will come back to you.

Oh—and call your mother more. She misses you but she won't
    say it because she doesn't want you to feel sad. Call her.

Cynthia, you might have noticed a pattern.
LOVE and GRATITUDE
They will carry you to where I am now—and beyond.

And finally, Cynthia, you are enough.
You are going to be more than fine.
Be brave. Be brilliant.

I love to look back at that letter from six years ago and see the wisdom in it, the encouragement, the self-love. I see how the discipline of running has carried over into my creative life, and how, by applying that discipline to my body, I have also trained my mind. (Mental strength, I've come to learn, is so much more important than physical ability.)

I also see the clues of what is to come.

I see the belief, the deep knowing that there is something

on the horizon. I see the encouragement to stop along the way and acknowledge the beauty of the moment. I see seeds being planted—of confidence, of reassurance, of compassion, of bravery—that will flower exactly when they are needed in the future.

Julia Lucas, my running coach, says the best strategy for a marathon is the 10/10/10 rule.

The first ten miles, you run with your head. You think about what you know, what you'll do, what course you're running. You don't start off too fast but settle into your own rhythm. I see this as corresponding to childhood in a life, that time when we are figuring out who we are and where it is we're trying to go.

The second ten miles of a marathon, you run with your legs. You lean into what you've been practicing, call upon your training, and come fully into your body. For me, this is like early adulthood, when we begin to apply all we've learned.

And, for the final stretch, when you think you have nothing left to give, you run with your heart. This is the rest of life, when we let go of everything and allow the strength, the muscle, the energy, the understanding we have built through the entire journey thus far take us across the finish line.

People ask me all the time, "How do you run that far? I want to start and I'm not sure what to do. I'm never going to be able to run that distance." They sometimes ask me the same question about singing or acting. *How did you get that far? I'm never going to be able to get there.*

The first thing to remember is that no one is asking you to run that distance, or even half that distance. No one is asking you to do any of it at all. The only person who can ask that question, and answer it, is you. All you have to do is just go outside and start.

That's it. *Start.* Put your sneakers on. Even if you only make it to the door, it's more than you did yesterday. Maybe tomorrow you'll make it to your front step. And the next day, maybe just down your street. It doesn't need to be half an hour, an hour, two hours. Five minutes of running is a run. A little bit is enough. And then, as you go, you'll find that your mind and body might start asking for a little bit more.

This is exactly what life is. A series of steps. You take one, then the next, and the next, and the next, and the next.

And soon, you realize you're running.

14

2

What Did You Love as a Child?

The seeds of who we truly are often are found in the memories of what we loved as a child. Take a moment and think of what you wanted to be when you grew up, or the thing that made you happiest before the world got involved. These loves—these desires—are our purest dreams, our clearest and most direct looks into our souls.

For me, that was singing.

My mum says I started singing when I was about eighteen months old. "Cynthia started singing when she wasn't yet two," she wrote in my baby book, "and she hums when she eats." I don't remember that, but I do remember the first time I sang in front of people. I was about five, playing a shepherd in the nativity play. They'd asked me to sing "Silent Night"—I don't remember why they asked me except for the fact I was not a shy child. But I do remember when I sang it, people stopped and clapped. I could see some smiling faces, and I remember feeling really, really good.

Like, sparkly on the inside.

I use that word because that's what it feels like when you're five. I still remember the feeling today. As if I were carbonated. I guess that set me off on a journey of doing more. Wanting more.

I didn't think I was different at all with my abilities. I just thought, *Oh, okay, I can do this*, and I assumed everyone else could do it too. But people seemed to like the way *I* did it.

After that, I began to realize that a stage was one of the few places I could feel that way.

Little me was bossy, bubbly, chatty, would sing absolutely everything, and was nosy—really nosy. I wanted to know about everything, be in everyone's business, and hear what everyone was talking about. I wanted to see what everyone was doing. I wanted to understand all that I could about the world. None of that was a bad thing, necessarily. When it was time to perform, this all worked to my advantage, and people seemed to accept these characteristics as helpful. But in other situations, these qualities did get me into trouble occasionally.

I was so curious about everything. Sometimes my teachers didn't know what to do with a fascinated student who asked so many questions. And sometimes others in my class seemed a bit intimidated by a kid who always wanted to know things.

There was one moment I remember really well. I was about twelve and my teacher told me to leave the class. She was getting annoyed with me—I was either asking too many questions or I didn't quite agree with her about something, I forget which. Teachers were often moving me to keep me from chatting so much. It was in English class, and what made this so memorable was that I loved this teacher, Miss Casey. She was amazing. Her breath always smelled like coffee and she wore a floral perfume I loved. Coffee and lavender. She wore necklaces and a big cardigan with flowy skirts. It was almost as if she danced or floated when she moved around the classroom.

I felt really seen when I was with her.

But on this day when she told me to go, I understood for the first time what rage was. In this moment, my anger burst out. "Why are you telling me to be quiet?" I asked, my voice raised. "I'm asking a question in class because I *want to know*. I'm not leaving! I refuse to leave. Why do you keep telling me to be quiet?"

What made that moment so painful was that Miss Casey was one of my favorites and this was the *one* time we didn't see eye to eye. I was so confused. I felt a deep rage because it was *her*, the one teacher who usually understood me.

And here she was, not getting me at all. That's what stung.

That was the day I first started to realize that for some people, I was sometimes too much.

I never felt that sense at home. I loved everything from

home. When you're a kid and your mother makes you food to take to school, some kids are really embarrassed. Not me! I thought, *Thank goodness Mum made some food and I'm taking it to school. This is what I would like to eat.* I was so proud of where I came from and of my mum and what she could do. Whenever we went on a school trip, it was the best because she would send me with a flask of jollof rice and some chicken. It's probably why today, even now, I pack little things with me, foods I enjoy so I'll feel that sense of being loved throughout the day.

But that day with Miss Casey was the day the word *too* suddenly entered my consciousness.

I talked *too* much; I was *too* loud; I was *too* nosy, *too* curious.

At first, this confused me and made me feel bad, but later, I learned that the things we get into trouble for as children—the *too*s—are early signs of our greatest adult strengths. The child who asks too many questions? She becomes someone who seeks to understand and solve problems. The one who's too talkative? She uses her voice to speak up for herself and others. That other one, who's too quiet and shy? He's simply observing and now knows how to interact with any kind of person. (And yes, the one who sings too loud someday finds her audience all around the world.)

It wasn't until I fully realized this that I saw myself more clearly and better understood who I've become, and why.

I asked questions and listened and got into everyone's business my entire life because I wanted to understand how people and life work, which is something crucial for acting and performing. I sing loudly because it's the way my voice knows how to make itself heard.

What if I had left those things behind just because I was told they were too much? There were times I almost did, and I can't imagine where I would be now if I had.

3

Be Vulnerable

Something else I learned through singing is vulnerability. Vulnerability is, in another word, openness—and when you sing, you have to be as open, literally, as you can possibly be. When we sing, we make sound waves come out of the very deepest parts of us. Those waves, then, have to be molded and shaped through space, through our physical bodies—and there is no space without openness. If you don't open your mouth only a muted humming sound comes out, which is fine if that's what you're doing, but to make a big sound, you have to open your mouth wide. And if you don't open your body while you sing, you won't be able to sustain your breath or your notes. All you will be able to pull from is what's on the surface, and that won't last very long.

Likewise, when you perform, the deepest parts of yourself become present, become visible, audible, and you have to be okay with that.

But that's not all. Once you sing, you have to add on to it. Not only must you open yourself up physically, you must also open yourself up emotionally, even when you don't know how others will receive it. You have to make clear your emotional connection to the music and give a piece of yourself to the people listening without knowing whether they will open their arms to receive it. You hope and pray they'll accept your gift, but you never quite know if they will.

Sometimes, the pieces don't work well together (and you won't know until it happens—a misplaced emphasis, a strain, or a gasp), no matter how much practice you put in or how good you are. There are simply just days when it won't work as you want it to, but you have to do it anyway.

That, too, is vulnerability.

You just have to go with it. You have to take the risk.

It's terrifying. But you have to do it.

And when it *does* happen, you feel it.

Every nerve in your body knows you've landed with the audience. There is a shift in the energy of the room. The walls are gone. The air is clear. Everything is wide open. It feels like freedom. It feels like what you're meant to do.

Vulnerability is powerful.

As is the Japanese concept of *ikigai*, having a sense of purpose and reason for being in life. It's about finding joy and fulfillment by aligning one's passions, strengths, and contributions to the world. It's what motivates me to get out of bed each morning and construct this amazing experience with purpose and joy.

Taken together, vulnerability and *ikigai* are formidable. And you can choose them for yourself at any time.

4

I'd Like to Lend You My Mother

Growing up, it was just my mum, my sister, and me. At home, music was playing in every room. Diana Ross, Lionel Richie, Phil Collins, Aretha Franklin, Bony M, and Nigerian music if my mum was in charge of the selections. In my room, R&B, Brandy, TLC, and Monica also rang out. Our house was a smorgasbord of music, all going on at the same time.

My mum loves music, and in her mind she is Aretha Franklin herself. As far as she is concerned, my talent for singing comes from her and, to be fair, I'm happy to let her believe that. And though it's not entirely true, she's earned those bragging rights fair and square. Still, one thing that is completely true is that she's not afraid of singing, which is absolutely wonderful. Can't you just feel the love that comes through when my mum sings around the house? Close your eyes and imagine it with me. A smile on her face, a little dancing to go with it. Bliss.

My sister was gifted with a lovely voice. She'll be so mad at me for telling you, but we're being honest here, so: *Sissy, the world must know!* We harmonized and sang a lot together, especially Disney songs like "Beauty and the Beast." Also, Kate Bush: "Wuthering Heights" and "Babooshka," as well as Elton John's "Daniel" and his duet with George Michael, "Don't Let the Sun Go Down on Me." Picture, if you will, the two of us, little girls by the kitchen sink, one of us doing the dishes, the other being welcome company, belting out songs to our hearts' content, unafraid, in the flow. Our own little concert. Royal Albert Hall, eat your heart out.

With music everywhere, home felt like a place I belonged. I could ask all the questions in the world and was never shamed for my curiosity. I could bring in as much music as I wanted and play it wherever and whenever I wanted. Mum would let me take over the hi-fi system and I'd spend an afternoon just sitting and waiting for a song I loved to come on the radio so I could record it. My passion for music was never, ever a problem.

I hope you had a safe place like that. But if you didn't, make one for yourself now, even if it's just in your own mind. That still counts.

Home is where I developed my deep and abiding love of music. It's one thing to sing, but it's another thing to *love* music. And I love music, not just as my job, but because it feeds me. Music is food and sustenance to me.

I also had an amazingly supportive mother, though she's Nigerian through and through. It's an odd thing for a Nigerian parent to say, "Yes, go and sing and be an artist." Almost unheard of! Most Nigerian parents want their kids to be doctors, lawyers, nurses, engineers. But my mum wasn't like that. "I just want you to do what you love. Go, do the thing that you're very good at."

That incredible generosity was hard earned from her own experience. Isn't that how it always is? Those of us who've struggled with a limitation really understand others in the same situation. In her early twenties, my mum wanted to move from Nigeria to the UK because her sister was emigrating, but her parents weren't on board. So she hid her sister's passport. "Send me with her or I don't give it back." They finally agreed, but her father was adamant she was to learn catering to support her sister. Mum, though, wanted to do nursing, specifically to look after children. Once in the UK, she did training in both catering and nursing at the same time. (Wonder where I get my ambition?) After that, doors started opening. She became a health visitor, focusing on the cognitive health of children and the mothers of newborns via home visits. But because she'd had to fight so hard to get to that place, she never wanted to be the parent who said, "No, you can't do this."

At some point in her climb, she met a man she fell in love

with and had me and my sister. Unfortunately, that man wasn't necessarily equipped for fatherhood, and so the raising and rearing of myself and my sister fell on my dear mum.

Mum, somehow in the midst of my father's iniquity—being mostly an unhelpful, absentee father—found a way to section off a piece of kindness in her heart. She made space in our lives for him and permitted him the chance to make space in his life for us. Neither of those challenges was of the sort he could easily rise to. He tried, I believe, to the best of his abilities, to be there, at least physically for us. But alas, failure was his destiny as far as we were concerned.

Mum's support, though, was ever present. There was a moment when I was about eighteen or nineteen when I just stopped singing and performing.

My mum noticed and said, "I just want to make sure you're still singing." She said it in passing, maybe walking to the kitchen.

The words reverberate in me still.

"I just want to make sure you're still singing."

That's a privilege a lot of immigrant kids do not have. A privilege, really, for any kid.

My sister, who looks so similar to me that she's stopped often by people mistaking us for each other, is also like Mum, with a career in health. She practices a sort of specialty sports science, encouraging restorative health using sports and fitness. She brings fitness regimes to those who are not used to being active, like those with diabetes, and encourages them every step of the way.

Perhaps this gives you a sense of who they are as humans—so helpful, so encouraging and loving. Good, kind people, the two of them. Every cell in my body knows exactly how blessed I am to have them in my life.

Who are you blessed to be surrounded by? If, unlike me, you're not lucky enough to have had a supportive mum or sister, just know that I'd like to lend you mine. Anytime. Picture them in your mind and allow them to love and champion you like they do for me. Oh, and I'm right here too.

Life is too demanding to go through without the love of an uplifting mother and a devoted sister. Or sisters.

27

5

We're Not So Different

I'm sure my biography is different from yours and yet, I'm equally sure we have so much in common. I grew up in South London in what was called a maisonette. The building used to be a church and though its facade stayed the same when it was renovated, small flats were built inside it. On our floor, my mother, sister, and I occupied Flat Five. Extraordinary, accepting neighbors surrounded us on all sides. Tayo in Flat Four with his two daughters, Clive in Flat Three, and Sharon in Flat Two with her sweet, severely asthmatic son, Benjamin. In the flat below us were two sisters, Samira and Safira. It was a miniature version of a council estate, with everything shrunk down because it was such a small building. That maisonette was also an astonishing, captivating blend of cultures that influences me to this very day.

What setting shaped you? What did you learn about the world around you from your early neighbors, friends, surroundings?

Everyone in our maisonette was an immigrant. We were Nigerian but Igbo, while Tayo and his daughters were Nigerian but Yoruba. Clive and Sharon and her son were all Jamaican. In this tiny building, my sister and I were awash in exhilarating cultural influences, exposed to just about everything.

When Mum went to work as a nurse, checking in on new mothers and their children, my sister and I would be watched over by these kindhearted, salt-of-the-earth neighbors. We might go stay with Tayo and his daughters for a bit, then head over to Clive and his adorable brown-and-black pit bull. At some point, we'd find ourselves staying with Sharon and her son, Benjamin.

By the time I was ten or eleven, I knew all kinds of different foods and different music. While both Clive and Sharon played reggae much of the time, Clive's selections were generally male led, while Sharon favored female vocalists. Tayo played Yoruba music and blasted British pop. His flat was where we watched our very first Disney movie; he was the only one who had a video player. Sometimes, Benjamin, my sister and I, and Tayo's daughters would all be in one flat together, so Benjamin would eat jollof rice with us, all of us a kind of made-up family, but a family nonetheless. It was here I learned the concept of "chosen family." Even if you weren't born into the family you wished you had, you could always choose a family of your own.

For me, this maisonette and the people in it provided the most wholesome, child-friendly upbringing I can imagine; it is the setting of my favorite formative memories.

I learned so much about the world in that little space because we were all so different and yet so similar. In that maisonette, I got to know Clive's short, stout, ridiculous pit bull. That dog helped erase my mum's own fear of dogs and helped to build my love of them. Where she came from in Nigeria, dogs were always kept outside and served as guard dogs, animals to be afraid of and to stay far away from. Initially, she was highly wary about this one, but my sister and I loved him immoderately and he loved us. After a while, as Mum saw the pit bull inside with us, guarding us and watching over us, she developed a new appreciation of dogs.

Sometimes that's all it takes to get over experiences or people we're afraid of—just spending time with them and learning to really see them. I now have two very sweet dogs of my own and whom my mother loves like her own, so much so that our calls are sometimes mainly to find out how Caleb and Gigi are doing. *When can she see them? When can they stay with her?* Growth.

Together in that maisonette, we all learned new ways of eating, dancing, and caring for one another—new, perhaps, and yet remarkably similar.

As a Black woman, it sometimes seems that the world uses the African diaspora to trick us into thinking we're all really different from one another. In Nigeria alone, the groups break down into Hausa, Yoruba, Igbo, and so many more, and though we all have slightly different traditions, we are really not all that different. So many categories try to convince us we're not the same. If you take a closer look, you will see that the line between us that is supposed to keep us different and apart from one another is faded and almost nonexistent.

Just look at food. My favorite Nigerian meal is okra soup. Now, if I go today to New Orleans and order gumbo, a uniquely Louisianan treat, it will be so similar to okra soup that they're almost indistinguishable. Both prominently feature okra, which acts as a thickening agent. Both are hearty, rich stews that often include a mix of meats or seafood, and both are served with a starch. (Okra soup is eaten with what's called a "swallow" starch, like pounded yam, fufu, eba, or ground rice.) Finally, both are typically made in large quantities, a signifier of community and tradition.

Meanwhile, over in Puerto Rico, they serve mofongo, a dish made with mashed green plantains, garlic, olive oil, and pork cracklings. While in Nigeria we have a yam porridge that's almost identical.

Those meals and many others, like the people who make them, come from the same or similar places.

Like our maisonette.
Like music, like laughter, like grief, like joy.
Food, people, music.
We're all a lot more alike than we realize.

6

What I Know and Don't Know

Fun facts about my father:

I don't know how old he is.
I don't know his birthday.
I don't know his profession.
I don't know his parents' names.
I don't know what his likes and dislikes are.
I don't know if he believes in God.
I don't know if he has a favorite color.
I don't know what his favorite song is, or who his
   favorite singer is.
I don't know where he lives.
I don't have his phone number.

Suffice it to say, I really don't know much about him
at all.

I was sixteen when he left me, alone, in a London Under-
ground station after an argument about a transit pass.

When he told me he didn't want to be in our lives
anymore, I stood there in shock. My head was empty.
No thoughts, just confusion and quiet. And then I walked
away.

The first step felt like running into a brick wall: pain.
Then: agony. My emotions opened like floodgates. I cried
so hard I could barely breathe, could barely see. It was only
when I ended up on the wrong train platform that I realized
I had been walking in the wrong direction. There, still in
tears, I corrected my course.

Just as I made my way to the right platform, there he was.
He was in front of me, walking straight in my direction. I
held my breath. Maybe he was going to apologize. Maybe
this argument would just disappear. Maybe he had realized
something was wrong, and was coming back to find—

Before my cascading scenarios could solidify into hope,
he passed right beside me. He made no eye contact, said
nothing.

I was nothing. A void, an empty space. From that moment forward, to him, I had ceased to exist. It was the last
day I ever spoke with him.

I do not know much about my father, but I do know a few
things:

His name
That he can whistle
That he always wore a leather bomber jacket
I think his drink of choice was a Tennent beer
His food of choice, a traditional Nigerian meal of
    ground rice or gari
with egusi soup or ogbonno soup.
We both have a gap between our two front teeth
and
by some strange stroke of irony
(and because God likes playing jokes)
My father can sing.

7

Magic Still Happens

I wanted to perform from a young age, and I kept finding ways to do so. When I was about eleven, a theatrical troupe came to my school to select kids to be a part of their summer program, and they picked me. We did an absurd musical version of Bertholt Brecht's *The Caucasian Chalk Circle*, and I played the Queen. It was the most magical experience. All we had was this blank room with no scenery, only sheets for a robe and a makeshift crown. But I came to see an important truth: Together, we had the ability to imagine and create something out of nothing.

We could simply do it with our imaginations. I could be whoever I wanted to be! Discovering my own magic was thrilling.

What magic did you uncover at a young age?

At that same time, I was beginning to learn that my singing was something I could control. I could use my voice and change the way things sounded and mess around. When I was conscious of what I was doing, I could change how people felt when they heard it. I started to have a real technical understanding of singing.

Mostly, though, I just played around. That's what the childhood years are for.

When I was fifteen, I went with a friend to an audition for *Romeo and Juliet* at a young actors' theater called the Young Vic, which was, unknown to me, renowned for nurturing young and emerging talent. It took the production that was being featured on its main stage and created a youth version. I was into drama and would have auditioned if I'd known about it and had time to prepare, but I didn't.

I just went along simply to be a supportive friend.

The director, Rae McKen, saw me. "Why don't you audition?" she asked. "You're here. You might as well."

"Okay, I'll try."

I wasn't prepared in the slightest, but I gave it my all.

And guess what?

I became Juliet.

This is what trying sometimes gets us. Not all the time, but if we don't put ourselves out there, we'll never know.

And that director, Rae McKen, years later became particularly instrumental in shaping my path. None of that could have happened without the attitude of "Okay, I'll try."

Where and when have you tried something new, even when not prepared? Did it lead you to risk more or to shrink back? You can always decide to try again.

What I remember most from that experience is the feeling of magic I found whenever I got to perform, whenever I crossed the threshold of a theater. It's something I chase and look for to this very day.

If, in your own life, you left the magic behind somewhere in your past, know that it's waiting for you to come back and claim it.

Magic is something that still happens. It's yours if you reach for it.

8

_____

See and Be Seen

I went to an all-girls Catholic school and had inspiring, amazing teachers like Madame Chesley, who made me speak French all the time. And now I simply adore that language. She seemed to have stepped out of the pages of a novel, and, to be honest, I had a little crush on her. She was this chic Parisian lady with wavy hair and round glasses and was very, very French. But oh, so kind and gentle. She took my love of French seriously. It wasn't long before she realized my skill was not necessarily in the writing of French but in the speaking of it, so she kept encouraging me to learn, to keep speaking. She is the reason I love French to this day. She saw my love and augmented it, teaching me to work hard to get what I wanted. How lucky I was to get this kind of intellectual and creative nurturing.

My music teacher, Miss Helen Rycroft, was absolutely

awesome. No one really understood her, but I got her. She would pretend to be this curmudgeonly teacher who didn't like people. But actually, under that hardened exterior, she had an amazing sense of humor coupled with what I can only call brilliance. Plus, she was so kind to me. Always kind. She figured me out right away: *Oh, I have your number! You are a musician. And I'm going to make sure you're always a musician. I see you.*

Isn't that what we all want, to simply see others and be seen by them?

Miss Rycroft accosted me almost immediately and made me learn to play the clarinet, partly so I would learn to read music, and then she got me playing viola. Whatever I wanted to try musically was open to me, though this wasn't the norm at my school. She wanted to make sure my hunger for music, singing, and performing was always fed.

I was part of the school choir, which did classical pieces. Miss Rycroft always gave me a solo, along with private lessons, taking me aside to learn about Schubert's lieder, or Handel, or Beethoven—always something to enhance my knowledge of music.

Together with Miss Asefo-Adjei—oddly enough, my science teacher—Miss Rycroft put together opportunities for us to sing with a big choir in the UK. Requiems every year, big choral pieces with all the voices. Tenor. Bass. Soprano. Alto. Mezzo-soprano. All those vocalists made such an immense, textured sound, blending and resonating off one another. Occasionally, there'd be recitatives in between, solo lines sung in the rhythm of ordinary speech. We performed long pieces separated into movements, like *Carmina Burana*. I get goose-bumps now just remembering.

The feelings of awe that washed over me when performing with the choir have never left. That memory pricks me with wonder and an acute awareness of just how stupefy-ingly beautiful music can be. It worms its way inside you and brings out feelings you didn't know you had.

Still, the path to our loves, to our passions, isn't always straight. Sometimes we wind about, looking for where and how we belong, where and how we can offer our gifts. Despite my aptitude and zest for music, it's kind of funny to admit now that there was a time in secondary school when I became obsessed with biology. I decided I wouldn't be a singer and an actress after all; I'd be a spinal surgeon! I was really good at science and saw myself as one of those kids who could have gone either way. I truly applied myself and was passing with flying colors. I liked doing well, getting good marks, and that propelled me forward. I can see now that I was trying to fit in. The other people in my class were all super intelligent, wanting to be lawyers or nurses or doc-tors or veterinarians. And I wanted to be a part of that, to belong. Not many people at my school wanted to be per-formers.

Actually, only one. Me. Only me.

Sometimes, following our own paths can be a little lonely,

and maybe we take a detour for a bit to enjoy the company of our peers. That's what I did. But eventually, the spine surgeon dream faded. In part because my teachers could see me so clearly and kept encouraging my acting and singing. The seeds that eventually blossomed into my career were planted by those teachers who saw me deeply and let me see them. I have such gratitude for every one of them.

Who are the people who have nurtured you? Those you've seen clearly, and those you've allowed to see you?

Who have you nurtured in turn?

9

Sing!

One of my favorite things to do is go back and listen to the John Rutter *Requiem*. I performed it in secondary school and I was so proud to be able to sing something that amazing and technical. And then, of course, *Carmina Burana*. We performed it in the chapel that belonged to the school. To me, that chapel was a huge space, but when you're young, everything feels huge. I'm sure it's much smaller than what I'm remembering.

Because we were in the chapel, there was this echo, and the sound would ring out and become absolutely massive. I loved singing *Carmina Burana* so much I couldn't wait for rehearsals, couldn't wait to be washed over by all the voices and instruments merging together, making something bigger than the sum of its parts. I was just so thrilled to be part of those tones, astonished that together we could make something so awe-inspiring and magnificent. It wasn't anything I'd ever experienced before: pure classical music. Prior to Miss Rycroft tricking me into singing it, I didn't even know I could make that sound. That it was mine to make.

Something else was going on, too, that I didn't realize at the time. What I was experiencing when we sang in the chapel was more than auditory. I was having a physical experience as well. Sometimes I see music in color. I'm not just hearing it, I'm actually seeing it. I'm also physically feeling the music, having a corporeal response to it. It's literally filling my body.

I didn't know what it was I was feeling, nor that it was unusual. I didn't have words to talk about it.

It took years to figure out. It wasn't until I was twenty and in drama school. There, we read *Musicophilia* by Oliver Sacks and I realized I was a synesthete. For years I had wondered: *Why do I have this feeling? I can't really describe what I'm seeing. I know I'm enjoying this experience, but it feels different from how other people are enjoying it. I'm having a different, maybe deeper, experience.*

Between ages of eighteen and twenty, I did a lot of backing vocals, singing in nightclubs, and still didn't realize what was going on. At one club I worked in regularly, the Arts Club, we would do a Florence + the Machine song. To me, whenever we sang that song, it was as if the room was covered in gold. I looked out and saw flashes of beautiful shimmering gold and yellow every single time we sang it. I couldn't get enough. I didn't know how to describe what I was experiencing, but I would ask to sing that song again and again. If it wasn't on the night's set list, I'd ask them to put it back on.

No one else understood. They all wondered what my fascination was. And I had no real idea. All I knew was that I needed to sing.

We don't always know why we're called to do something. We just know what that insistence feels like in our solar plexus. And we know how to answer "yes."

10

No Vocabulary for Love

In the family I was raised in, queerness wasn't discussed. I think my closest friends may have known I was queer for a long time, maybe even before I did.

I feel like I knew it when I was around fifteen but didn't know what to call it. I didn't have the vocabulary. I just knew I was attracted to both men and women. I was simply attracted to people. I'd have a crush on this person or that person. Like the synesthesia, I didn't know how to put it into words.

It all became devastatingly clearer in secondary school. I had a crush on a girl and didn't realize that's what it was. We were always crushing on other girls in our year, but this felt different. This girl and I made plans to get together for some outing and then she wasn't there. I waited and waited. I thought maybe she just lost track of time. Eventually she showed up really late and I didn't bring up the fact I'd been waiting for ages because I didn't want to displease her. I tiptoed around what had happened so she'd want to spend more time with me.

Then she asked me to meet her again. The second time, she left me waiting even longer, an hour and a half, maybe more. The realization that I was being played with hit like a thunderclap, a wake-up call.

"I'm gonna go home!"

I left before she arrived and made a commitment to myself. I was never going to put myself at her mercy again. It took a while to realize that I had fallen for her, that I was following her around as if I were a stray puppy dog.

I found that attraction worrisome. I didn't talk to anyone about it because I didn't know how to describe it.

I was also afraid.

Nobody was talking about queer sexuality in my friend group, and I couldn't talk with my mother or sister about it.

I couldn't because I was too scared. When you're young, you know without being told when something is seen by others as "not good."

I'd spent my entire life trying to be as good as I could, and now I worried. What if some intrinsic part of who I was would never allow me to accomplish that goal, would doom me to being "not good"?

47

So I buried my sexuality after that experience in secondary school. It was only later in drama school that I started to talk with people I cared about, friends I felt safe around, to ask just a bit about what I was feeling. I put a toe in the water to ask others about what they felt inside, to see if it was possible to own this part of myself and still be "good." At the time, I was still exclusively dating guys. I don't think I dated a woman until my late twenties.

Gradually, piecemeal, slowly, I came to see I was who I was and began to accept myself. To own myself fully. That was the first step. When we are okay with who we are and others have a problem with it—that's *their* problem, not ours. Still, it took me time.

And even more time before I was able to talk with my mother and sister about my queerness. I didn't want to be spurned by them. After all, I'd already lost my father to rejection. I didn't want to risk losing them too. But we finally did talk and that felt good and freeing, as if I was letting them fully see me in the clearest light possible—even if it didn't lead to the full-throated acceptance I'd hoped for. At least, not initially.

It's a conversation we approach with care, a territory we're still navigating.

My queerness goes against the grain of what many people think is right and proper; I think my mother is worried about what others think. But she is coming to the understanding that what others think doesn't worry me in the slightest. I know she's trying. I see her working to reconcile the idea of what she had in her head for me, her plans for me, and then working to let go of those plans. I'm aware that must be hard. She knows I'm my own person. That I get to choose who I love. She's starting to see the fact that my queerness is an additive thing. It doesn't take away from me. It's the cherry on top of who I am.

It's simply more.

With my sister, it's taking us longer, but we've recently come over a bit of a hump, finding our way toward each other. We've come to terms with the fact that I'm just being myself, and I want her to be as much of herself as she can possibly be. For us, it boils down to this: If I allow you space to be fully yourself, I will ask for that same space for myself.

We're getting closer as a result.

We used to avoid the hard conversations, but now I tell her, "If you ever have questions or want to talk about these tough things, let's do it. That's the point of being sisters. It doesn't mean I love you any less, or you love me less. It just means we're consistently working through our things and growing together."

In some ways, it means we're allowing each other to be simply more than what the other might have envisioned.

I have room to check myself on whether I'm allowing a person I love to also be more.

My sister is one of a kind; she's special; her brain is brilliant. She's shy. Loving. Unbelievably creative; she makes her own cosmetics and they're good! She's a passionate adventurer and solo globetrotter. The truth is I admire her, and I should tell her more.

49

Is there someone in your life who's asking for your blessing to be their full self? Can you grant them that grace?

Or maybe you're afraid to be fully yourself with a special someone in your life. Can you take the chance? Leave the door open that they might surprise you.

11

Learn from the Boring

During the day, I went to university and studied music psychology—essentially how music affects the mind or the psychology of a person, why a minor song makes us feel sad or a major song makes us feel happy. I learned how music affects our social standing and what it does to us in social surroundings. I wrote papers about what happens to a person's mind when they listen to music, how the synapses carry emotions, how the tears come.

But at night, as I was in the nightclubs doing backing vocals, I could see with my own eyes what music did to people. One day, it hit me. For a year and a half, I had studied and asked questions and read and passed exams. But I wasn't learning anything I didn't already intuitively understand. I was not stimulated by what I was doing. *At all*. Everything was fine, but I was bored. Bored out of my skull. Not learning, not connecting, not feeling.

Nothing.

The voice came again: *This isn't right. This is not what we desire.*

So, I listened to it. I left university, determined to find something that sparked.

Another step.

Another lesson.

If it's boring the life out of you, it's not your life.

12

Take the Nudge

While in university I spent a lot of time at my local theater, the Stratford Theatre Royal in East London. If moments are seeds in our lives, and there are places that become the soil where they grow, then Stratford was that fertile earth.

I got a job at the theater so I could spend as much time there as possible. I worked every position I could: front of the house selling tickets, serving drinks in the bar at intermission, being an usher. I did everything. I also watched every production, mesmerized, completely enthralled. And over time, my desires sharpened and became really clear. I watched the actors on the stage. They were singing and playing characters, with costumes and lighting, making that magic that had sparked in me as a child.

Oh, my God. This. This is what I want to do. I want to be there, on that stage!

Around the time I quit university, the theater was getting ready to cast a show called *The Harder They Fall*. I worked up my courage and asked if I could audition.

"No," they told me.

I was completely devastated. "Why not?" I asked.

"Because you don't have the experience and we haven't seen any of your work."

"I can do it. I promise I can."

My words fell on deaf ears.

I was determined to change their impression of me, so I signed up for a Young Actors Company course being held in the theater. The day the course started, I was standing in the ticket office, getting ready, when two people came in. I knew most of the people who passed through the building, but one of this pair now standing before me was immediately recognizable as someone from my past. I was shocked.

It was Rae McKen, the person who'd directed me in *Romeo and Juliet* five years earlier. She knew what I could do. She'd seen me act. And as it turned out, she was the one teaching the course I was about to enter. I'd had no idea when I'd signed up.

Rae remembered me and, before the course even started, pulled me aside.

"Are you going to train?" she asked.

"Train?" I didn't know what that meant and told Rae as much.

"Will you go to drama school?" she clarified.

I wasn't even sure what drama school was.

"It's where you go to train," she explained. "If you want to be an actor, you should go to drama school."

I had never thought of such a thing and even with her nudging me, I didn't know how any of that could be possible.

I didn't know how anything worked in this world; I had sung, of course, but no one had ever suggested I formalize my performance desire through study. I wouldn't know where to start.

"I think you should go to RADA," Rae said. "The Royal Academy of Dramatic Arts."

My response was immediate:

No.

It wasn't going to happen—mainly because the school had the words *royal academy* in it. No Black girl from South London was going to get into the royal academy of anything.

"That's a nonsense idea," I replied. "I'm not going to do it."

Rae stood her ground.

"Well, if you don't apply, then you can't do this course," she said.

My jaw dropped. "What do you mean?"

"If you don't come to my office this afternoon and apply to this school, you're not coming to this course."

I agreed to apply. I really wanted to do the course; I knew that being in the theater was where I belonged. But I was also annoyed. Highly annoyed that she was making me do this.

Are there people in your life suggesting a path for you? What would happen if you took their nudge?

At the time, I didn't know that thousands of aspiring actors applied to RADA every year, hoping to get one of the few spots available. Auditions were held not only in London but throughout the UK, Dublin, New York, and Los Angeles. It's one of the world's most competitive drama schools.

I'm glad I didn't know that because I applied to RADA and I didn't apply anywhere else. Just to spite Rae.

13

Enough for Everyone

I was invited to audition for RADA and made up my mind I stood no chance. I was still cross I was having to do this to placate Rae, but I might as well see it through. It would be a good experience with auditioning. I held zero dreams that this was what I wanted, what I needed. I purposefully dressed down in tracksuit bottoms and an easy top paired with a head wrap. I was not going to invest myself in something that was impossible.

But who knew? I was invited back to a second audition. I still didn't get my hopes up. During that audition, I was asked if I'd apply to other drama schools or reapply next year if this didn't work out. By now, I'd come to understand just how competitive this path was and how many people ended up re-applying or attending their second- or third-choice school.

I knew the correct answer. Of course I should say "yes" to show my commitment. The word was all formed in my mouth, but that's not what popped out.

"No," I said and was greeted with utter silence. "I don't want to go anywhere else." That was my truth, but all the auditioners laughed.

I worried I might have messed up, but later came to see that exchange in a different light. Perhaps I provided the auditioners with one of the only honest moments they had that day. I was telling the truth only because I thought they weren't going to take me, but it seemed that being fully myself was actually disarming. And attractive.

I further realized my ethos at work was already becoming solidified even if I couldn't fully see it yet. I'd presented my real self, tracksuit bottoms and all, because I was sure I would not be accepted. But in their eyes, I was there dressed to work. The things I assumed they would count against me actually seemed to work in my favor when I was authentically myself.

For the final audition, we were all going to spend a whole day seeing how we worked together. I was given a speech to prepare and present before the other aspiring actors and the faculty. Another woman was assigned the same speech. She was asked to present before it was my turn. She started speaking the lines and then her face betrayed panic. She was going blank on what came next. Without thinking, I fed her the next line. It was just automatic. *Here's one line and there's a second line*. Soon, she was back on it and finished her speech, doing very well. My mind never went to the thought that if perhaps she failed, there'd be more room for me. That I could maybe shine with the very speech that had been her downfall. It was just natural. I needed to help her out.

And that, too, became cemented into my work ethic. Because, as it happened, both she and I were accepted into the program, reminding me of a vital truth:

There's enough for everyone.

Can you be authentically yourself, tracksuit bottoms and all, and trust there's enough for you too? Try it. See if that attitude can become yours as well.

14

When I Doubt,
I'm Always Proved Wrong

Saturday morning.
Early.
My curtain was still closed
and the day was sunny when
The artistic director of RADA called

You did really well at the auditions and I'm wondering
If you would like to be a part of this year's intake of
the Royal Academy of Dramatic Arts

Are you serious?
He paused.

Like, is this for real?
Yes, he said.

I couldn't believe it.
The acceptance letter came a little later.
I tried to wrap my head around what was happening.
I was sure I would not get in

By no means will this school be perfect for me
It doesn't have to be perfect to be your path
Still, it's the beginning of an understanding that
When I'm fully myself
I'm at my best.

When I doubt whether I can do something
I'm always proved wrong.

15

Sometimes,
They Don't Understand

There were thirty-four people in my RADA class. Four were Black. I was one of them.

Though I had hoped to love the experience, and I did benefit greatly from it, there were also many uncomfortable moments and many times when I wondered why I was there.

If you find yourself in a place where it feels like you don't fit, breathe your way through it. Sometimes it's true that the path is simply uncomfortable. The discomfort doesn't mean it's not yours.

At RADA, for example, there were a lot of microaggressions and misunderstandings. Many assumed I was aggressive, and that the characters I would play—and would want to play—would all be the Strong Black Woman archetype.

Anything else, it seemed, I was deemed unsuitable for. There were assumptions that, because of my talent and my abilities in class, I didn't need the help everybody else needed. A terribly short-sighted misconception.

In some senses, they were right but not always. What they also failed to understand was that I had a single mother, and so I needed help in other ways. The support I needed was frustratingly financial.

The first year, I asked for time off to perform backing vocals for a group, a job that would pay my entire three years of tuition. The school's registrar, a woman named Patricia (or Pat as she was known) denied me the two weeks I requested, but the school let another student, a white boy from Eton, do a play over the same period. He didn't need the help I needed, but he was given the time off without question and without consequence.

To make my way through, I kept working, but I was forced to do so on the fringes. The school day started at eight in the morning and didn't finish until six or seven at night. When we were doing shows, the clock inched closer to nine. Five days a week, I finished at RADA and then went to do evening gigs to keep bills at bay. Sometimes Saturdays and Sundays too. I was falling asleep in my classes from overwork.

Later, after I finished my studies, I found myself reflecting on my experiences, my resume, my opportunities, and I realized they'd been punishing me. I'd been given the smallest roles and the least amount of grace. I didn't quite know why, but (because I'm a big mouth) I decided to ask the artistic director. Whatever he might say or I might say was not going to necessarily matter—I had an agent now and no longer needed their help—but I still wanted to understand.

"Why had I been given so little?" I asked.

"Well, that first year, you wanted to go off and do backing vocals," he said. "We didn't think you were a hundred percent committed. We didn't feel like you were ready for the large roles."

I was angry and frustrated. I explained to him why I'd needed the work. That two-week gig could have saved me so much stress, so much worry. It could have offered me hours I didn't sleep, peace I could never quite achieve. It would have paid for everything in ways they would never know.

They didn't understand.

This is a reality I have come to accept. Sometimes people don't understand, and we need to do our best despite those circumstances. We can triumph even when others don't get us. We have that power.

16

And Maybe They Never Will

The realization that some people will *never* get us came to me only recently, some eighteen or more years after the fact. It happened when Patricia, the woman at RADA who'd denied me the time off, wrote to say she'd heard me talk about it on TV.

Her recollection of what had happened was completely different from mine. "You felt it might be a good move to leave RADA and take the opportunity to go professional," she wrote, misconstruing what I believed had occurred. She said she'd asked me why I'd wanted to abandon my training to be in a backing group when, if I stayed at RADA and completed my training, I would have every opportunity to be the star performer. She then ended the email by congratulating me on my decision-making prowess. "Good choice!" she enthused.

Her email floored me. I found it deeply condescending, with no admission that a mistake had been made. I had simply been asking for time away to offset my tuition costs. As it was, it took me years to pay back the fees because of that decision. I was left with the consequences, though at the time, I had been given no choice. Yet, she didn't see that. She recalled a silly child about to throw away a prized opportunity. At the time, she had dismissed what I'd proposed as not important when it was deeply important to me. The truth was, I had never had a single thought to leave RADA and here she was, congratulating me on making a good choice when I'd had no choice whatsoever in the equation. I wrote back and tactfully, I think, clarified what had happened.

I want to make something very clear.

I needed to go to work.

I needed the money.

I was told not to.

And for three years after that, for merely asking and then having to find some other way to support myself, I was punished for it.

Whichever way history is rewritten, those things are facts.

And here's the takeaway: Lots of people will not get us as we work to be just more. We have to let go of their perceptions and do what's ours regardless.

Some people will get us. Some never will. That's just the way it is. Don't lose sleep worrying about those who don't understand.

17

Look for Your Helper

During that time, though, there was one person who got me.

Joan Oliver was a lovely northern Black woman who wore the biggest smile (and really cool glasses). From my earliest days at the program, I believed she must have pled my case when I was auditioning—she had been one of three people at that table, and she'd seemed to recognize me.

Well, maybe not me, specifically. But me, a Black girl from South London who could do amazing things but didn't know it just yet.

Over the three years at RADA, we'd talk with one another, and for years after, we texted from time to time. I still have her number. She was my caretaker, my helper. She guided me through.

Who has been in your corner? I know someone has.

Even now, I can see Joan sitting at that table, watching me as I sing. Her eyes seem to say, *I recognize this girl*.

As I keep singing, I believe that's what Joan is thinking. I can hear it, louder and louder, in my mind.

I recognize this girl.

I keep singing, and I keep working. No, the others do not understand. But one does. And as I keep running further down the path, I hear her voice begin to meld with mine.

I recognize this girl.

18

The Seed May Be Buried Deep

I was twenty years old and an outcast at RADA. I'd always felt different, but now it felt less like a feeling and more like a fact. I actually wondered regularly why they all seemed to hate me so much. I was given tiny parts and didn't feel included. Was actively overlooked. I kept my own counsel and did my work but was awash in loneliness and confusion.

Then, suddenly, there was another student, a friend—well, he soon became a friend—named Michael Pivoy. He could play piano. He spotted me. He *saw* me.

"Do you want to sing some stuff?" he asked me one day.

I did.

He picked up a couple libretti, and we went to a little room with a piano. We played the music for hours. He kept asking me to sing one song, from one specific show, over and over and over again—a song about a girl and a wizard, about hope and belonging.

We sang the whole show, front to back, everything.

I learned the libretto like the back of my hand.

I learned the whole score years before I even saw the show.

It was the first time at RADA I could take a big, deep inhale and exhale. I could actually breathe. I was not pretending. In that little room, I was not trying to be anyone else but myself. I could just sing as me, and I knew I was not being judged. I knew who I was in that space, with a person who just liked my voice and liked me, and all that was requested of me was to sing. He loved the sound of my voice. I liked the sound of his playing piano, and I liked how we sounded when we sang together.

It's as simple and huge as that.

Somewhere, deep inside, as the crescendo built, the seed was buried deep where it would bide its time. For a decade and a half, many roles and opportunities would come, but not this one. Not yet. It was waiting for the right moment to take root.

Unlimited. My future is . . . unlimited.

19

Learn to Own What's Yours

As my training at RADA came to its conclusion, all the third-year students began to study their musical numbers and mount productions, preparing for the endless run of showcases and screenings they hoped would catch an agent's attention. I already had an agent, was leaving school early, and didn't need to worry. But that didn't mean my hard work was recognized or rewarded.

When it was time to cast the musical, *Company*, once again I was given a small, insignificant role. By this point, I was not surprised. It had become clear where I stood, what they thought of me.

The other girls were given large roles. I will not describe what they looked like. I think you already know. I no longer cared.

As the date for the show approached, I was told that two of the girls had gotten sick. One had laryngitis, the other food poisoning. They wouldn't be able to sing. There was a fairly straightforward solution: take them out and ask me to cover their roles. It's what anyone normally would do. It's the responsibility I was prepared to take on.

Instead, I was asked to sing backstage for the sick girls.

That's right.

I would sing while they lip-synched on stage.

The powers that be quite literally took my voice away from me and gave it to someone else.

When we rehearsed, I knew in my body this wasn't right but didn't know what to do about it. It wasn't until the first performance that it really hit me. I was being kept hidden while these two girls took the stage. I was having to use my voice—what's mine in the deepest, most intimate sense—to sing for other people. I was being erased while these two were benefiting from my gift, the ability I'd worked really hard to develop.

Why had I agreed?

In that moment, I realized I hadn't really had a choice.

I was devastated. Humiliated, actually.

I would never do this again.

By the time I handed back the microphone, I finally knew what was mine. I was ready.

I stepped away from that place and fully into myself.

Sometimes, knowing what is not for you opens the door

to what really is. Maybe it's time to hand that microphone back.

Oh, and now, in a strange turn of events and because God loves to play jokes on me, I am the vice president of the Royal Academy of Dramatic Arts. I can't tell you where those other ladies are, and frankly, I'm not sure I care. I know if they ever need someone to supply the voice while they lip-synch, it won't be me. Unless by some strange happening they end up as contestants in *RuPaul's Drag Race* and need to lip-synch for their lives and it's my song they compete to. In which case, may they not fuck it up . . . but I digress.

73

Part Two

———

Run the Second Ten Miles with Your Legs

In this segment of a marathon, it's time for the runner to lean into her training and rely on what she's been practicing. In life, this is when we put into practice all we've learned, when we start to make real strides. This is when we start to come into our own.

20

Look for the Clues in the Now

It's always interesting to look back at the past iterations of ourselves. At the time, we don't believe much will change. From that time and place, a naivete envelops us and we really can't imagine a future that is much further away from our now. If you look back five or ten years, would you immediately recognize the you you've become?

Me neither.

When I reread that letter I wrote six years ago addressing my future self, I thought back then I could see so much about what was coming—and to some degree, I could. But I was also a little blind. I couldn't fully envision how big my life might become. The me I am now knows that the me I was then wasn't being all the way honest with herself. That previous me thought she had reached her peak. And perhaps she had, for right back then. At the time, she believed she'd already experienced the best the universe had to offer.

Little did I know.

I remember writing that letter on what was a beautiful day, with no idea there were days waiting for me that were even more beautiful. Just as there would also be days filled with hurt and anger and frustration. This is the human condition; nothing remains the same. But on that beautiful day, time did not freeze itself in place. No, it rolled right on and took me with it.

I imagine when you look back on days past, you'll find you were not able to fully fathom ever being where you are right now. And yet, if we really looked, we'd find small clues of where we're heading. They're often hiding in plain sight.

Just a thought. Look for those clues in the now.

21

What You're Drawn to Is
There to Enlighten You

I saw *Wicked* on stage for the first time on my twenty-fifth birthday. I'd saved up to buy tickets to a few West End shows as a present to myself: *The Lion King*, a stage version of *The Lord of the Rings*, which was really beautiful, and *Avenue Q* with the Muppets.

Wicked was startling and breathtaking. I had sung the music for years, and now the entire show—lights, music, voices, sights—was unfolding in front of my eyes, filling my entire being. I was lifted by the music and transported by the story that was so deftly staged. When the flying monkeys came into the aisle, I felt like a kid. *Oh my God! What the heck?*

That experience seared itself into my being. And yet, for as much as I adored seeing the show, and for as much as I'd found singing that very music downright irresistible for years, I didn't really picture myself ever playing Elphaba. I didn't dare dream it.

And that's for one simple reason. I had never seen someone like me in that role. My brain didn't make the connection that such a thing would ever be possible. It's hard to become what we don't see. Even though Elphaba is green and it shouldn't really matter, it did. At least, in my head. By that time, the show had been open awhile. If, over that span, no one like me had ever played the role, then it was off the table. Not that I wouldn't have loved the opportunity; just that it wouldn't ever come my way.

Being cast for certain roles was always like that for me. I'd think, *Well, I can play* this *role, but I can't play* that *role.* Roles for Black women were few and far between, full stop. You're limited. Or, that's how I saw it. You can be a singer in this show, but you won't be speaking. Or you can be a day player in that show, but that's it. You might get hired for a television procedural where you're one of maybe two Black people, or you're the best friend. There's a cultural assumption of what's available to you. But really, you're most restricted by what you allow in your own imagination.

Are there areas in your own life where you've limited yourself?

I can see now how much my own constraints held me back.

But only for a time.

Despite that, I felt a deep connection to Elphaba. I recognized in her the feelings of someone who's different. I'd always been able to recognize other outsiders like me, and I got that about her immediately. We shared a deep feeling of kinship.

Much, much later, I'd come to see the parallels between us, but I didn't make those connections at that time. The weird relationship she has with her father is almost too close to the bone. She's so young, and she's looking for her father's approval and wants so desperately to be loved by him. It's obvious they have this toxic and not very loving relationship. It was all too similar to my own life. And yet even as I watched it unfold onstage that night, I didn't see it.

Maybe that's because the feelings were still too disagreeable. Sometimes we can't see what's right in front of our faces.

Of course, a lot had to transpire in my own life to dilate my imagination, to stretch it big enough until I could see myself as a potential Elphaba. By then, I'd begun to eschew the culturally imposed race restrictions I had experienced. I also made tentative peace with my past and could finally allow myself to see many of the correlations between myself and the green girl. This transformation was still rather vague in my head, a thought here and there, until the day it settled into my body—and I would never be the same.

By then, I'd been cast as Elphaba and we were filming the Ozdust Ballroom scene. I was using all the tribulations Elphaba was going through to understand her character. They were essentially all the challenges I had faced. Feelings of rejection and loneliness and shame. I was aware I shared the outsider status with her. I also understood the allegory of being green and how her skin color made her different, like how I'd seen myself due to my own skin color. Still, I didn't bargain on connecting with her on the father and sister relationships side of things.

But in that scene, she becomes quick and self-protective, pushing people away. And the understanding hit me with a deafening crash.

Oh, I've lived this before. This is familiar. Very familiar.

I was overwhelmed by that awareness. It was almost too much.

This is about someone who feels different, who feels alone and not as connected with others as she'd like.

This is about someone like me.

In that moment, I realized I'd been doing exactly the same thing—for years. I'd been singing this exact music when I didn't feel I belonged and, in response, wanted to push people away. And while it was nice to connect those dots, making sense of why I'd been singing the music for so long, filming that scene was hard emotional work.

But that's what life asks of us, especially those of us who are wanting to be simply more. There's work to do. And then more work.

Still, the experience left me overjoyed. I saw for the first time how all the pieces fit, and I finally realized I wasn't insane. There'd long been a reason I'd been drawn to that music. There were very good reasons I'd hidden in it and been able to find solace. So much made sense. My life seemed to click into place.

But that recognition was still years away. When I saw *Wicked* on my twenty-fifth birthday, I had entirely adored the experience.

And silly me. I thought it had absolutely nothing to do with me.

Be patient when you don't see where and how all the pieces fit. Just know this: What you're drawn to is trying to show you something important.

Do Not Give Them a Reason to Say "No"

It's a lot easier to limit yourself than to dream big. Sometimes we place limitations on ourselves because we feel safer that way. And often, other people will place limitations on us, too, so that we can serve as the reason they don't have to expand themselves in turn. They feel more comfortable staying small.

Do not let that happen. At every crossroads, question why you think something you desire is not for you. It's usually fear that is stopping us.

But when we push against that fear, when we question it and really examine it, the fear often melts like a snowflake in the palm of your hand.

. . . .

I have always been a big dreamer and there has never really been a different version of me, though in some ways, I've had to grow into my knowing. Now, I have a precise clarity with myself.

This is what I want.

I want *this*.

The first thing I knew I wanted in that deep, intuitive way was *The Color Purple*. I knew the show was coming to London and that it was going to be staged in this tiny two-hundred-seat theater, the Menier Chocolate Factory. This piece could have been for no one, but that didn't matter to me.

I simply knew I was supposed to do it.

My gut and my heart knew, but unfortunately, the people casting the show didn't.

They wouldn't see me. I think they assumed that a Black girl who'd gone to RADA and had done a commercial comedy musical could not possibly connect to the character, Celie, a poor African American woman living in the rural South, deeply oppressed, quiet and submissive, shaped by trauma. They didn't realize I was a Black girl who'd been raised by a single mother, who'd put herself through the Royal Academy of Dramatic Arts by working every waking minute of her life, who was from South London. Just like when I was a student at RADA, I had to recognize that sometimes people won't understand you. You can't let that stop you.

I became like a dog with a bone. I was not going to give up. I was a runner determined to get to the finish line.

I got my agent to badger the casting folks—and still no audition. Then a friend, Jason Penny Cook, who'd been one of the mentors of the Young Actors Company and had seen what I could do, stepped in. He talked with the artistic director of the theater. *Hey, you should really see this girl. Like . . . just see her.*

Not long after, I got the message. Yes! They would see me. They sent over four scenes for me to prepare as well as one song from the show, and I was asked to prepare another song. I had only two nights to learn the material, not very much time at all, and I thought to myself, *Were they trying to trip me up so they wouldn't have to deal with me?* One less aspiring actress. They could simply dismiss me and move on.

But I decided that was not what was going to happen.

This was what was going to happen: I was going to learn this material like the back of my hand. I was not, under any circumstance, going to give them a reason to say "no."

At night, in bed, I went over the scenes in my mind—over them and over them and over them, learning the material as thoroughly as humanly possible. *The Color Purple* had been one of my favorite movies, one of my most beloved books. I held on to the narrative of trauma and resilience and hope, reviewing all I adored about it.

. . . .

The evening of the audition, the director, John Doyle, was present, along with the artistic director, the music supervisor, and the producer sitting in the back. The lights were low, not bright. Nice, perfect. I walked in very much myself, nails done. My nails were light blue with fluffy white clouds on them, looking nothing like Celie at all. I had just come offstage in a different production and they'd have to take me as I was. I did the assigned scenes.

Then the director, a really gentle older Scottish man, disarmed me with his questions.

Tell me about yourself, where you come from. Who your parents are.

My mum raised me.
    My dad disowned me.
    I put myself through RADA because I love singing and
    I love the idea of being able to join music and acting together.

Huh. Okay. Now sing the song, please.

When I finished, the music supervisor and artistic director were both crying. I left the audition thinking maybe it went well. Hoping it went well.

A month or two later, I was doing a little play called *Lift* at the Soho Theatre when I got the call. I had the role. I was so very excited. It's all I wanted at that time. To do this show at this tiny two-hundred-seat theater.

I didn't know where it would lead.

We never do know. Still, we need to follow.

To this day, I still don't know why I was so determined to get that part. I can't say it was just because I loved the play, though I did. I adored everything about it. What it stood for, the characters, the music. But more than that love, I just knew I needed to do it. At that time and place, it was what God or the universe needed from me.

I could almost hear a voice telling me: *I want you to do this thing and be in this place because this is the door opener for you.*

Sometimes, we feel ourselves pushed to do something and we have no clue why. All of a sudden, there's this thing we're drawn to.

Why this? Why do I care so much?

Forget the questions. Don't worry about the genesis of your drive. Trust your instinct. Shoulders back, head up, breathe deep.

Because later, we always find out why.

23

The British Don't Do That

The Color Purple sold out every night
The people who came to see it were over
   the moon
It was like a mania
Every night people would stamp on the floor &
Get up in the middle of the song "I'm Here"
It was wild
I'd never seen an English audience respond this way
They're usually very mannered and restrained
Let's sit back, wait, let them finish
Let everyone get their work done and then we'll
   applaud
Not for this show

They were stamping their feet & offering standing
    ovations
The British simply don't do that . . .

And yet every night
It happened again and again

24

Happy by Any Means Possible

The British press didn't give *The Color Purple* great reviews. One complained it wasn't violent enough. In the London version, I'm thrown on the floor by Mister and shoved to the back of the wall many times, and that wasn't violent enough? They complained Celie didn't get grayer over the course of the show. She goes from age fourteen to forty-five. How gray did they want her to be?

Truth be told, they wanted her to look decrepit at the end. They wanted Celie downtrodden and devastated.

That's because it's easier to manage and disregard someone whose spirit has been destroyed.

But I knew she was determined to be happy, by any means possible.

Any means possible.

. . . .

I think there's a misunderstanding that anyone who is going through traumatic events, as Celie is, actually wants things to be that way. Maybe we think they've brought the misfortune on themselves. Either way, we're pretty sure they can find absolutely no spark of joy given what they're experiencing. Maybe they don't even deserve joy.

That's a pretty sad and one-dimensional perspective.

For me, even more heartrending is the person who's determined to find delight despite the horrors of her circumstances.

That's Celie.

Celie is on a mission to find crumbs and smidgens of happiness with whatever's unfolding. She finds amusement and comfort with Sofia, who embodies resilience and the desire for justice. Free-spirited Shug, who is beautiful and independent, awakens Celie to love and its many forms. Celie also experiences joy in her own cooking.

She is a magpie, ransacking her life for shiny moments to take her out of this world. And there's so much we can learn from her.

When Shug shows up, Celie is happy, relieved, even. *If she's here, then I might be fine.* With Shug's presence, Celie discovers a bit more freedom. *I want to go to the juke joint. I want to listen to music. I might not be able to join in right now, but I'm definitely going to watch people dance and sing.*

If Celie wasn't constantly trying to find uplifting twinkles in her life, her story would be unrelentingly, desperately sad. And though it does get very dark, that darkness is meaningless without her determination to be delighted.

But that's actually how life is. We laugh to keep from crying. Joy is often the best way to heal hurt and pain.

So when the critics seemed to want her to be more beaten down, I realized the power of Celie's quest for joy. It is nothing short of subversion. Like laughter in the face of pain is rebellion. Friendship and actual love—showing these qualities to others—is downright revolutionary because we're so used to seeing the opposite. We're often drawn to drama, tension, confrontation, raised voices. Many of the top TV shows thrive because they show us the worst versions of people.

In that light, Celie makes no sense. Why would this small Black lady who is being abused have any reason to smile? And though we think she shouldn't smile, she still has the muscles in her face to make a smile. She's young, and there are days coming that might be a little bit brighter. This is a person who has learned to live moment to moment to moment to moment and notices *everything*. Being present and observant, she finds scraps of beauty and happiness and delight that would otherwise be overlooked.

It's why she can see flowers. It's why she can see how scared Shug is. It's a skill she has honed. She notices that Shug doesn't eat that day, but she'll eat if Celie makes the food. Or that Sofia really doesn't like when people say a particular word or call her a name.

I admire people who are consistently in the moment and always seeing those little things. If there's a pattern in the roles I pick, that might be it. Each of these women is really good at observing.

Aretha Franklin noticed everything. It's why she couldn't bear to be in a room when she didn't like whatever was happening there. She'd simply turn on her heel. *I'm not staying.*

Holly Gibney has that observant quality too. It's a part of her DNA; she can't help but pay attention. She sees everything in minute detail.

And, of course, Elphaba and Harriet are attentive.

When you're an outsider all the time, you're busy watching everything and everyone. It's the best way to be safe. People are busy not talking to you while you're busy watching how they talk to other people, figuring them out. And by noticing your surroundings in such tiny specifics, you can't help but find sparks of radiance and glee.

If you look for them.

This is what makes Celie's stance so infectious and endlessly powerful. When we are determined to be happy despite what life offers, despite today's circumstances, by any means possible, it's absolutely seismic.

We become a force to be reckoned with.

What are the special things you noticed during those times you were overlooked? What have you seen that others have discounted?

25

If It's Yours, You Cannot Stop It from Coming

Fluke of all flukes, a reviewer from the *New York Times*, Ben Brantley, saw the show at our tiny theater, something that never happens. What he wrote in response was not really a stage review. More of a love letter. And that love letter changed everything. Suddenly, the producers wanted to take the show to Broadway.

Broadway!

When *The Color Purple* first opened in that little theater, I was asked at the time if I'd go with the show, should it make it that far. I thought it was a joke.

Sure, I'll go . . . I mean, if you'll have me.

I didn't take it seriously.

And now, it was a very real possibility.

All along, I'd allowed myself to be led by my curiosity, to fully feel my determination to grow and strive for what I wanted. And strangely enough, those very qualities were what now seemed to be opening doors and portals for me, passageways I could hardly imagine for myself. The more I leaned into vulnerability and receptiveness, the more goodness came to pass.

Openness is what expands your life, your center.

Still, it isn't always easy and takes a long time and unrelenting determination to get here. Don't get me wrong. I've had a lot of big, giant knocks, rejections, and hurts along the way. We can't expect not to when our dreams are big.

But listen: If you allow the experiences that come to you to keep revealing the different pages of who you are, if you refuse to let the negative words stick, if you stay open and growing, if you refuse to shrink inside yourself, your path will keep revealing itself. You just have to take the next step.

That's what I'd been doing, and now, the brightness and reality of Broadway beckoned. I learned from a fellow cast member that the director said he did not want to do this show in New York without me.

Without me. The girl who was hidden backstage at RADA. The girl who was only good enough to be heard and not seen. The girl who was always supporting, never the lead.

Broadway.

If it's yours, my friend, you cannot hold it back.

26

Like Candy Floss on Your Tongue

With opportunity comes change, and let's be honest. Change is not always comfortable. Even when it's change for the better.

I was now leaving home to follow my dream. I wasn't just moving to another city or country. I was leaving the entire continent, twenty-six years old and not altogether sure I could do it. My knees were shaky and I was a little afraid. I didn't believe it was actually happening until we started to organize my ticket.

My mum was really proud of me. But I have to say, she's never once been surprised when amazing opportunities come my way. It's as if she's just been waiting for this moment. Even when huge accolades that stun me come over the horizon, she doesn't bat an eye. I think the only thing possible that might have surprised her would have been if I'd become an actual spinal surgeon. Her perspective on my career has always been, *Well, of course this was gonna happen. You do whatever you want to do.*

Those words have been in my head forever.

Whatever you do, just make sure you work hard and do it well.

Now as I prepared to leave her, she made sure I had what I needed to move abroad. None of us really understood what was happening until I left for the airport. My sister saw me off at the door.

I'm not crying, she said.

I'm not crying, I said, both of us lying.

My mum and best friend took me to the airport, and we were all just a mess. It wasn't until that moment that it hit us all. I was leaving. I figured I'd just be gone for the length of the show.

What I didn't know at the time was that I was leaving to begin a whole new life. Something was being born in me that I hadn't even envisioned.

I was pursuing a dream that felt as ephemeral as candy floss on your tongue.

I've come to see that's how it often unfolds.

27

Be Open to What Might Be in Store

Before we opened on Broadway, I had no expectations of how the show was going to unfold. Like so much in life, I had to put myself and my heart out there, not knowing how they would be received.

We'll see what happens.

People might like it.

People might not.

We might open for a week and then shut down.

There was no way to know.

That first night, we were connecting with the audience, and it seemed to be going well. I was used to doing this play in that tiny London theater, but now there were nearly 1,200 sets of eyes watching me, and it felt intimidating—and wonderful. I could hear the audience breathing, then holding their breath. I could see into the eyes of some. I felt their attention. I felt their presence and was so grateful for it.

We got to the penultimate song, "I'm Here," the place in the show where the London audience reacted so strongly. I was standing alone on the stage, not expecting anything out of the ordinary because this audience didn't know the London history. They were coming to this play as blank slates. Maybe the only reason people had overreacted in the West End was because they'd heard it had happened the night before, and the night before that. People had perhaps come to expect that reaction and thus created it. So I didn't think it would happen in New York.

But I was wrong. So very wrong.

Before I got to the final bars of the song, it was happening again. People were standing, stamping their feet. The entire theater.

I was used to it in the small theater, but in this one, it was deafening.

The applause was absolutely deafening.

The whole place was on its feet, but we weren't finished with the show yet. We had another fifteen minutes until the end and I needed to keep the narrative moving forward.

Someone was supposed to enter here? Wasn't there a line that was to be spoken?

What was I supposed to do?

And though I was worried about moving things onward, I also wanted to be mindful and conscious about how people in the audience were feeling in the moment. It was important to allow them their emotions. So I just held character on the stage for a moment or two and let the applause rain down. Throughout, I wordlessly told the audience that the person standing in front of them was not an actor playing a character, but the character herself.

I was Celie.

In my own head, I was telling myself over and over, *Do not break character!*

I slowly turned away. By giving the audience my back, I was able to communicate, *Okay, we're moving on now.* It was not a scripted moment, but it did what was needed. I soon heard a shift in the response, a tiny quieting. Only then did I begin to move. I languidly picked up my sheet. Next, I picked up my glass. The audience got the message. People settled down. There was still a little chitchat, but it was lessening. The applause didn't stop instantly, which was actually quite lovely, but now people were ready for us to continue.

I'm really not sure how I knew how to handle that moment. I was so new, and it was my first-ever experience on Broadway. I suppose it was intuition. Plus, I have to say, kindness.

Throughout, I was thinking about the other people in the show who were waiting to come back on the stage. I needed to set that scene for them.

What's my job here? To be aware of what is happening in the moment, but also to be aware of what is going *to happen.*

The audience still had some traveling to do. I didn't want

anyone to feel like this was the end because it would short-change whoever was coming on next. We moved past that moment and all was well.

And then the next night, it happened again, but now I knew how to handle it. Night after that, same thing. The show ran fourteen months, eight shows a week. More than four hundred fifty performances in all.

As a result, I was nominated for the Tony Award for Best Actress in a Musical. I was utterly astounded and couldn't believe that the young girl I had been, who so needed to prove herself, who'd been so afraid of always being an outsider, whose talents had been overlooked in the past, had warranted this kind of attention.

Whose life was this, and how had it become mine?

Funny enough, my mum was completely unfazed when I told her. She simply wondered what she was going to wear.

I won the Tony, as well as an Emmy and a Grammy for *The Color Purple*. I couldn't believe it.

And yet for me, the awards themselves aren't the goal. It's the opportunity to perform, to create, to make magic. *That's* the real joy. The awards are an after-the-fact confirmation that our performance touched hearts. I'm so grateful for every one of them.

And while I know this may sound outlandish coming from me, who, from the outside, it might look, was handed so much, I know the awards are not why we do what we do. We do what we do because we have our gifts to share.

All of us do. Each of us are artists in our own way and what we offer—maybe the world's best apple pie or an amazing, intuitive way of being with friends—is of value even when there are no awards ceremonies to celebrate these offerings.

All of which raises questions: What do you hope to gain from what you are doing? If recognition would change you for the better, make you more willing to take chances and give more fully of yourself, can you simply provide yourself with that recognition?

Consider this your own personal award: my individualized acknowledgment of your talents. I want you to go and fully do that thing you're good at.

Don't wait for the reward. The life you're living and the life that is waiting for you are the rewards.

28

Every "No" Is a "Yes"

After my father abandoned me
I spent years trying to prove myself
Learning instruments
Singing everything possible
Running
Achieving
Knocking myself out
It took a while to learn
His "no" to me was in some ways a gift
He gave me the space I needed to say "yes" to myself.
When I could finally stop trying to prove myself to
    him
I found the core of who I am

I could say "yes" to me
And that was an even better "yes" than the one
I'd been hoping for from him
One that resonated in my bones and allowed me to
   become
Simply more.
So when parts I want don't come my way
When rejection stings
I hold on to this:
Every "no" makes space for an even better "yes."

29

How Big a Life Are You
Willing to Live?

At each stage of life, a transition comes. It's like we're walking down a hallway and at the end of it, we are faced with
two doors. One leads to a bigger life. The other leads us back
to the familiar, to safety, to smallness. Over and over again,
we're confronted with the same questions.

Do I want to keep growing?

Am I willing to do the work?

What do I need to fortify myself to move forward?

After *The Color Purple* closed, I found myself flying a lot,
going state to state, performing gigs, giving concerts, vis-
iting new and unfamiliar places. Isn't this what I'd always
dreamed of?

But now, getting ready to leave for the airport, I'd found myself awash in anxiety. My heart pounded, sweat dampened my underarms, my hands trembled. I kept worrying.

What would security be like?

Would there be lines?

Would I get there in enough time?

I was a wreck.

I'd always thought I'd go home to London. That was the deal I'd made with myself and what I had expected to do. But now, opportunities kept beckoning, one after another. I kept saying yes, thrilled. Until it was time to leave for the airport again.

I'd never been an anxious flier.

And now, this new fear.

What was going on?

As I thought about it, I realized I would either have to get over this anxiety or scale back my dreams. Those were the only choices left to me. And that's when the reality of what was happening struck.

With every flight I boarded, I was literally traveling farther and farther away from my past, from what I thought my life was supposed to look like, from my family, from my home. Every trip to the airport showed a new and not altogether comfortable truth.

I wasn't going back to London. Not anytime soon.

What I was actually doing was building a new life in the States.

No wonder the airport scared me. It was proof of this

new, bigger life taking shape. If the fear could convince me not to fly anymore, then I'd have no choice but to go home. To stay put. To shrink into a more manageable-sized me.

I came to see that being in an airport as often as I was meant I was afforded a luxury I'd never had before. That of being in an airport often. My life was getting bigger.

The only real question was, would I allow it to keep expanding? I honestly am constantly asking the question of myself now.

That's how I found myself in therapy at twenty-nine, driven by this anxiety. And there, once we'd dispatched with the airport anxiety, I uncovered things—memories, resentments—I didn't know I'd been holding beneath the surface. Over time and with help, those issues were addressed. But not solved.

Nothing is ever solved.

Still, they went from screaming at me to just nudging me a bit. The distress I felt on a day-to-day basis, I came to see, was the result of what I'd experienced and buried a long time ago. What a blessing! When you start to understand that your actions are connected to things you've been through—events you've never discerned or excavated or explored—you start to find yourself getting a little bit more space.

Being abandoned by my father had put me on a hamster wheel. That was the root. I was constantly trying to prove myself to others.

That I was worth loving.

Worth taking up space.

That I was good enough.

You cannot sustain that behavior. You are, essentially, doing all that work for someone who has no idea what you're doing. But in time and with my therapist's help, I found I was being less hard on myself. This habit has not gone (once an addict, always an addict) but it's certainly not as extreme as it was. Realizing what had long motivated me meant I could leave it behind. Today, when that old "prove it" thought comes up, I can check myself. I can refocus on my true purpose.

I was starting to demonstrate to myself, finally, blessedly, at long last, that I was enough.

Once you know that, the scope of what you're able to see is far wider and broader than before. The world becomes bigger and there are more things for you to do in it. Therapy was a portal. By asking for help, I opened my hands to receive this bigger life.

And so now the question comes to you.

How big a life are *you* willing to live?

30

Allow Yourself to Be Seen

Part of being a performer is allowing yourself to be seen and to connect who you are to the character or to the song. This may seem antithetical to what we do. If I'm playing the role of this other person, shouldn't I be hiding myself so that the other person shines through?

The opposite is actually true. In inhabiting the characters I play, it's my humanity, my heart and soul, along with my body and voice, that bring them alive. The things that make me *me* are the things that help me share who the characters are as people.

Soon after I left drama school, when I began auditioning, I would look around me and realize everyone, myself included, would show up to the auditions dressed and looking as close as possible to whichever character we were auditioning for. I don't know, it didn't make sense to me; it felt like we didn't trust the panel of people in front of us to see us transform without anything but the words we had been given. I realized then that hair played a big role in disguising us, hiding us. I didn't want to hide anymore. I wanted to present myself with the challenge of transforming with nothing but me. A change was necessary. It was time to allow people to see my face, to actually meet me.

I said to myself, *I'd like to walk into a room and have people just see my face.*

That was the starting point.

I met with my hairdresser for the dramatic cut I envisioned, but the hairdresser would only cut some of it. I left the salon that day with a cut I didn't want. I'd allowed that person's fears or projections to shape how I made my decision. A week later, I marched back in there with new clarity and intent. I explained exactly what I wanted and this time emerged with the radical cut I'd desired, one that told the world my beauty didn't stem from how I did my hair.

Hair is such a fraught subject for many of us and I found myself freed up emotionally once I embraced this new look.

I tried it blond for a while and then an auburn color at some point. It got progressively shorter and shorter and shorter. I would grow it a little bit, and then I would color it, and then cut it even shorter.

When I came to New York to do *The Color Purple*, I struggled, not having a regular stylist on that side of the Atlantic. So I grew it for a little bit until I found someone who would help me cut it down.

It wasn't until *Wicked* that I shaved it completely. What liberty! Now I do it myself.

And while the genesis for this change had been my desire to let others see me, I thought back to those auditions when we all looked the same. I realized I wanted to be simply more.

I kept remembering back to being a child and playing the Queen in *The Caucasian Chalk Circle*. We'd had almost nothing—a sheet for a robe, a makeshift crown, no set—and yet we'd been able to conjure magic. I wanted to go to those auditions and do the same. I wanted them to see the alchemy I could generate.

I adopted a uniform for auditions: sweater and jeans, flat shoes, and basically no hair. What you see is what you get. That really changed things for me because it meant I was comfortable when I got in the room. I was relaxed. And the casting people could really see what I was doing.

Oh, she transformed! I can see her standing in the character's dress without her having to do it for me.

No artifice, nothing.

I use my voice, my body, my movements to bring the character to life in your mind, not props and makeup and costumes. This is an actor's real strength, and by removing the other pieces, I allowed that metamorphosis to be visible. I myself am just the blank canvas on which it occurs.

But the truth is this:

When people look at me, I want them to fully see me.

Can you allow yourself to be seen as you really are?

I promise you, it's utterly transformational.

31

Be Willing to Be Surprised

Life is full of surprises. We can view them as potential threats or welcome them as yet-undiscovered delights. It's interesting that feelings of fear and excitement often feel similar in the body: a flood of adrenaline, a rise in the heartbeat, a flush in the chest. When those feelings come over me, I name them as excitement, if at all possible, and I'm often amazed by the surprises that are in store.

Other roles in dramas and musicals came my way and each was an honor to embody. It wasn't until I got to the end of *The Color Purple* that I felt well equipped to tell Harriet Tubman's story, both physically and mentally—because it's a feat to do both those things. A certain kind of mental hardiness and physical stability were needed to be open enough to tell her truth.

By that time, I'd readied myself. I wanted to make sure people saw her as a real, breathing, living human being. Harriet: her small stature, a woman, Black, vulnerable to being underestimated. But inside, immense strength and courage. I felt an intense sense of responsibility to protect her story and to emphasize the importance of her legacy.

Viewers already knew her as a superhero. Harriet Tubman is an icon like no other, but I wanted to make sure people understood that she was a young woman first, someone who once had desires. She fell in love and then fell out of love, and was heartbroken. And that's really the reason she went back to Maryland the first time—for her husband. I loved the idea of being able to bring her humanity to the forefront so that people understood it wasn't an easy thing for her to keep going back. It wasn't ever easy. Every time, she had to actually put her life in danger. And she did this simply because she wanted to share the experience of freedom. She wanted others to experience it with her. That was the thing I was chasing after. Telling her human story.

And then, Aretha Franklin, another American icon, a hero for me in many ways. My mother used to play her music in the house all the time, but playing the woman herself included daunting moments, especially learning her habits. Her vocal choices were always fascinating because they were never, ever predictable. It all depended on what the song was and how she was feeling on the day she sang it. I was enthralled with her. She's such a singular person, and the life she led was not all roses and flowers. Still, the way she channeled what she experienced into her music, into her writing, was intimate and powerful and distinct. She connected like no other person to the music, and somehow always managed to make whatever she had to work with her own. She might do a gospel song, then a song with George Michael and Annie Lennox and Lauryn Hill. Her creative reinvention was endless. I adored that about her.

I hope I made her proud with my portrayal. I really wanted to. She's one of those people who deserves to be celebrated. She put out so much work and touched so many. And she's truly one of the few artists known around the world by everyone. It doesn't matter where you're from. I could ask someone from almost any country on this globe about Aretha Franklin, and they'd know her.

And the surprise, for me?

Aretha earned me an Emmy nomination for Outstanding Lead Actress in a Limited Series or Movie, and I was nominated for an Oscar for both Best Original Song and Best Actress for Harriet. I own those accolades and was so grateful for them. Added to the wins of *The Color Purple*, I was three-quarters of the way to an EGOT at thirty.

At the time, it felt a little wild. What on earth was happening? How was this going so fast? I was completely surprised.

But since then, I've been teaching myself to be as present as I can. I want to simply go with the flow. Whatever comes to me, I let happen. I want to be there when it's happening—not just afterward. I used to have this habit of only seeing these things after the fact. *Oh, my goodness, that happened?* And now, what I desire the most is to always be present. I want to live for the surprises—and really, everything is a surprise.

Hopefully, I'll still be open to surprises of all sorts way into the ripe old ages of my sixties, seventies, eighties, nineties.

What are the accomplishments in your life you have trouble remaining present for? Can you commit to seeing them fully, to appreciating them? Can you allow yourself to really feel how special you truly are?

32

Don't Tell Me About It Unless
It's Meant for Me

I firmly believe that the experiences in life we're meant to have will find us, and if it's not meant for me, it's best I not know about it. I held on to that idea when I heard the movie version of *Wicked* was in the works. I knew they were seeing people for the film and I told my team to not say anything to me at all.

I don't want to know. Don't tell me anything unless it looks like it might come my way.

Deep down, I knew I would have loved to be part of the film. But if I ignored what was happening, maybe I'd be able to protect myself from being hurt if the part didn't come my way. I kept telling myself, *If I'm not connected to it, if I know nothing about it, I can go about my business. I don't want to get my hopes up only to have them shattered.*

And by keeping myself in the dark, I was able to stay focused on what I was currently doing, not become distracted by shiny things that might never come to pass. Either way, I still had work to do and had to simply buckle down to it.

Then I bumped into the director, Jon Chu, at an event, and we talked.

So, we're doing this film, he said.

I heard. You're directing? Great!

We discussed the part of Elphaba, who she was.

It was a really gentle, genuine, generous conversation, just talking, no pressure.

We met a second time over Zoom and I told him what Elphaba meant to me and what I could possibly bring to the role. And then he went away.

I repeated my edict to my team. *Don't tell me about it unless it's for me.*

They said, *They might call you in. It looks like they might call you.*

Don't tell me about it unless it's for me.

Then the call came: They wanted to see me.

I may have been the last person to be considered for the role.

Perhaps this *was* for me.

119

33

Train Like a Boxer

When big moments come to us in life, sometimes we only recognize them in the rearview mirror. But at other times we know exactly what's happening in the very moment it transpires. The experience is lit up in neon lights, telling you, *This is the way. Keep going. You're getting there.* And when that happens, it's time to buckle down. Focus in. Work.

That was how I felt with *Wicked*.

I had three weeks to prepare. A far cry from the two days I had for *The Color Purple*. Things change. I got the music and all the scenes and started working on them like I was in training. As if I were a boxer. There's a discipline to being an athlete that crosses over to just about every part of our lives: We set goals for ourselves, look for progress over time, trust our legs and training to carry us, and don't give up. Nothing really happens without a major commitment on our part, a commitment to see things through. We refuse to trust chance or rest on our laurels and the fact we've done well in the past. Rather, we set aside all that's extraneous to fully prepare. We must become our best selves in the time allotted to us.

As part of my training, I ran while singing the *Wicked* songs, back and forth, singing just to get them fully into my body. I wanted the music and dialogue to all be so deeply embedded inside me that when I got to the audition I wouldn't be thinking about lyrics, or the melody, or lines. All that would just be a part of my DNA.

I ran the lines constantly. In the shower, I sang the songs over and over and over again. On the day of the audition, I even swam laps trying to sing the songs while swimming.

With every week and day and hour and minute that passed, I brought myself closer and closer to being ready to do what I knew I could do.

To becoming Elphaba.

I arrived early for the audition and for the first hour, it was just me on my own. I practiced with the pianist, a luxury to have before an audition. He was lovely and played with emotion and patience, which is sometimes rare at an audition.

I felt really grounded. I showed up with no frills, just me in a T-shirt and jeans, a pair of comfortable sneakers—or was it a pair of flats? I forget . . . Oh, and I wore a red knitted cardigan because it was soft and cozy and I wanted to feel comfortable. When I am at ease in my body, I am able to be relaxed in my art.

It was important I wasn't thinking of anything other than the work when the time arrived. And that's what happened. I did not think of myself at all. Only Elphaba. Channeling her.

Before one of the songs I was to sing, Jon asked about my connection to Elphaba.

And though I'd thought these things over the years, I'd never before given them voice.

This was the exact piece of music I escaped into when I was in drama school. If I was having a really bad day, or was miserably aware of how odd I felt there, an outsider who couldn't connect with the others, I would hide out in a music room with my friend Michael. We'd sing this together. We'd stay in that little room until the very last minute before we had to go back to class, belting our hearts out. This song gave me refuge. Singing it during a very vulnerable time in my life, these songs made me feel safe.

I got emotional telling him this because it was the first time I'd told anyone how alienated I'd felt. How alone. How freakishly weird and not part of the mainstream.

That's the feeling sometimes, I've come to realize, of being simply more.

Yet singing that music had given me sanctuary. I'd felt safe. And I'd come to feel Elphaba in my soul.

When I finished speaking, Jon asked me to sing. And you couldn't have told me that in that moment I wasn't wearing Elphaba's cape. That I wasn't holding her broom.

Every emotion, every nuance, it was all alive inside of me.
Her broom was my broom; her green skin, mine. My voice
was hers. It all came together. I felt alive.

And that's another clue in life:
    When you feel *that* alive
    You're doing exactly what you're supposed to do.

34

Don't Play with Me, Jon

After, it was a hellish few weeks
I don't want to hear about it! I kept saying
But inside all I could think was
When are we finding out?
For God's sake, please, when are we finding out?
I was in London, biding my time, working
Anticipating
Is it happening?
Is it not happening?
Have I got it?

I got an email from my team
They had a book they thought would be a good project
    for me

We should jump on a call, they wrote
It was one a.m.
It can wait, I replied
Then I got a text from my agent
We should jump on a call now so we don't lose it
How did all my team know I was awake?
Why were they asking me to get on a call at this hour?
But they knew me
I *was* awake and could take the meeting
I was in my pajamas, but who cared
It was just my team, and I dress up for bed.

I put on a pair of glasses and set myself up on the sofa
When I logged on, Jon Chu's name came up
But not his face yet.
What?
My first thought was that
He was also interested in this book.
The minute his face appeared on the screen
We both laughed
I was still not figuring things out
Are we here to discuss this book? I asked
Who's leading this meeting?
Nothing was connecting
Nothing. At. All.

Then Jon started to talk about this girl in drama
    school who

When she felt out of sorts, would go to a room and
    sing
One day, she walks into this room and starts singing
    about this green girl
The pieces fell into place
Don't play with me, Jon, I warned.
I was too afraid to believe
Don't play . . .

I don't know what fucking planet you come from, he said
But I think the rest of the world should see more of you
I lost it
We want you to be our Elphaba
All I could do was cry
I put my head in my arms
My glasses flipped up
over my head
gulps of air and tears streaming
All I could say
thank you very much

A wild moment
For me, the culmination of a dream I didn't even
    realize I had until
I was in the situation of wanting the dream.
Only later would I realize it was ten years
almost to the day
Since I'd first seen *Wicked* live in London.

The seed had first been planted
Twenty years old and at drama school
Nurtured on my twenty-fifth birthday when I saw the
    play
And even then, I couldn't imagine I'd ever be
    Elphaba.
And now,
ten years after that,
that seed was finally
ready
to
fully
bloom.

                                                                         ———

127

What's the dream you don't even know you have?   ———

35

Make a Pact

Life is hard, and even harder when we make up our minds we're going to do it by ourselves. We don't need anyone. We can't trust anyone. Get out of my way.

I did that for a while and it wasn't fun. I have since discovered the lasting pleasure, creative thrill, and deep satisfaction that comes in making art with others, in investing ourselves in relationships. In trusting.

All that energy came to the fore as we began work on *Wicked*.

Jon Chu hosted a gathering for those of us working on the movie to meet, to get to know each other. Me, Winnie Holzman and Dana Fox, who cowrote the screenplay, composer and lyricist Stephen Schwartz, Stephen Oremus, music director and arranger Marc Platt, our glorious producer, and of course, Ariana Grande.

Jon Chu, our prospective maestro, was a gracious, friendly host, and he put everyone at ease immediately.

"I want to welcome everyone," he said. "We're about to go on this great big journey together."

He'd been working with Paul Tazewell, the costume designer, and had laid out a table of what the costumes might look like. He also had trays with little yellow brick roads for each of us. We signed them so each would have one signed by the others.

We had dinner together and then someone suggested Ari and I sing one of our songs with Stephen Schwartz accompanying us. This was the moment when Ari and I would hear our voices together for the first time.

Singing with someone you've not sung with before is an intimate and vulnerable thing. You really do have to open yourself up to that person to fully hear them and be open to allowing yourself to be heard. Then, you combine your voices.

We had not practiced. We had not sung this song together before, and we were about to do it with others present to hear us.

A risk. I didn't know if our voices would fit together. I was a little nervous.

We took deep breaths, smiled at each other, and opened our mouths.

A sound came out, and it was this amazing blend of the two of us. We were startled and tickled but continued to sing.

Our voices are very, very different, but when we sang together, we discovered this harmonious blending—Ari called it "worming"—the way we sort of found each other. It was astonishing. Our two very distinct voices somehow found each other and became one.

It just worked.

We felt it. The others felt it. Magic was happening.

There were tears. We were both speechless.

That night seemed an indication of where the rest of this was going. If we could sing like that without having done it before, if we could make magic with absolutely no practice, if we could combine our voices this powerfully in front of a room of people—with nothing, no makeup, no costumes—then we could really do this. We could follow the yellow brick road wherever it would lead us.

To make sure we stayed on that road, though, before *Wicked* really started rolling, Ariana and I made a pact with each other. We committed to protecting and caring for each other through this process. We hear often how female costars—or really, any costars—can sometimes let their egos get in the way until they battle each other, destroying the creative process for everyone involved. We were determined to do the opposite. To be the opposite. To build on each other's strengths, to encourage the other, to see if, like our voices, we could become more than the sum of our parts. We were two women determined to become simply more—with the help of the other.

Day to day, we made decisions together, always moving together. It was never "I'm over there and she's over here." No, we worked in tandem.

We were always looking out for each other. Our partnership was important. We shared a strong synergy, a commitment to authenticity, and that, combined with the natural connection we fostered both on and off set, allowed us to support each other emotionally and professionally.

If there was a particular scene coming up, say, and I needed privacy and alone time, she would advocate for me. *Hey, she needs some quiet.*

Or if Ari had a particular need, I would advocate for her. We both needed different things at different times. When there was a lot of emotion we were working with, Ari needed to connect. She needed to be close, so I sat with her and was present with her.

If we were working on set and both of us felt like we needed a break but we didn't want to be running away from us, from what we were building together, we'd discuss it.

Should we ask for a little time away?

Yes.

And then we'd ask together: *Both of us would really love a break, if that's possible.*

We took responsibility for working together in the most supportive way possible and throughout, we were having conversations. Sometimes, that meant being vulnerable about difficult situations. If I'd had a bad day, I'd discuss it with her. It wasn't necessarily the prettiest conversation, but she was open to listening to me. Just as I was open to hearing her too. If something was going on that she wanted to discuss, we talked by phone, or I went over to her, or she came over to me.

We were there for each other, not just for the good moments but for those that were a little more complicated, a little tough. The fact that we were consistently there for the other, over time, built deep trust. And that trust and togetherness created a level of honesty and intimacy that allowed us to actually make a film as special as this one.

This degree of intimacy was necessary and we consciously built our relationship with each other not just for *Wicked*, but for outside it too.

We were two distinct human beings, two women, learning to work with and trust each other. Just as part of *Wicked* is a story about two women learning how to love each other, so we practiced the same in our own lives, on camera and off.

We made each other family.

And now our chats have become a constant recitative. We speak or text each other almost every day, even if it's just *Hey, have a good day* or *What's going on?*

We committed to living through the ongoing back-and-forth of life with each other.

That, I have since come to appreciate, is genuine partnership. We were determined to defy the stereotype of two women working together—bickering, catty, competitive. We aligned with each other.

Is there someone in your life you can make a pact with, to care for, to be kind to, to support? Life is hard enough as it is. Commit to helping another person, and let that person commit to helping you.

133

———

Part Three

Let Your Heart Carry You the Rest of the Way

For the last 10K of a marathon, it's all in the bank. You've done the hard work. Now feel your expansive, tender heart pulling you forward, carrying you over the finish line. One foot in front of the other. That's all it takes.

36

This Is Why You Do It

We do our work and hope it has an impact. Day after day we show up, try to be the best version of ourselves, share the gifts we're here to give, and join in the stream of life. Sometimes people tell us we're too much and maybe, on those days, we can't help but wonder if it really matters, if it's worth all the effort.

That's okay. Keep going. Keep running. Take the next step.

Because sometimes hard days are also amazing opportunities.

I'm thinking of the times I had to fly for *Wicked*. While those moments were deeply thrilling and absolutely exhilarating, they were also physically intense and sometimes punishing. Your body goes through a lot.

Though it might not look like it on the screen, the reality is, when you're flying, *you're* going to be doing a lot of the work. Say I need to do a loop with my body. People may think that the crew member operating the wires, called a papa joe, will do it for me, but he and the wires simply take me from point A to point B. I'm the one who has to flip my body into the actual loop. Like so much in life, though we may need others' help, we have to do the hard things for ourselves.

On those days when I was figuring out how to fly, I was busy determining where to place my weight. Sometimes, it went horribly wrong and all I could think was, *I don't know how to do this!* I kept trying different things, falling, failing, messing around.

It reminded me of a quote from Samuel Beckett. "Ever tried. Ever failed. No matter. Try again. Fail again. Fail better."

All that sounds so noble and above the fray, but Samuel Beckett likely never had to deal with chafing from a harness.

Chafing: It sounds funny until you experience it. The reaction to "You get a lot of chafing when you're in a harness" is usually a chuckle, laughter. What actually happened was that the harness rubbed on my skin so much and so hard and so long, over and over again, that the skin on my hips started to burn off. Chafing is no fun. Being in a harness for hours does other things to your body as well; your skin gets pulled every which way. Then add flying into the mix and singing while doing all that. It was a lot. And it was sometimes grueling.

On a daily basis, I was bruised. I definitely had a bloody nose at some point. I broke my nails. I kept landing on my knees and even lost feeling in the skin of my left thigh, a strange sensation.

But after hours and days of failing, something clicked. I realized, *Oh, I have to put tension in my hips and my legs as I bring them round behind me in order to fly in straight.*

You learn by doing, and somehow figure out the aerodynamics along the way.

One day, ten-year-old Karis Musongole, who played young Elphaba, came to the set. I was in full makeup and she was just enamored with Elphaba. Whenever we could have time together, I made it a point to see her. It wasn't a lot, but it meant something to me to be in the same space together with the girl playing the younger version of me.

This one day, we were shooting a scene. "Would you like to see me fly?" I asked her.

She said she would.

They brought her in by the monitor. I was going to do a descent, nice and easy. She saw me being taken up by the wires and asked, "How does she land?"

I could overhear her being told, "You'll see . . ."

And as I was flying in, I heard her little voice in echo: "Whoa!"

139

That's it, just *whoa*, but it contained the world.

Her wide-eyed amazement and astonishment, her awe. Marvel, complete surprise wrapped up in the kid innocence of unbridled imagination. She was playing the little version of Elphaba and I was showing her what was possible. Despite the fact she'd seen me being taken up on the wires, she still believed I was flying.

She actually believed.

And if I could fly, maybe she could too.

The next time my hips were abraded and my knees bruised from my flailing efforts, I remembered that moment.

Whoa.

This is why you do it.

37

No Small Days

The day I flew for Karis would seem, on its face, a small day. But it wasn't because there are no small days. I used to say that to Ari: "None of this is a small day. Everything is a big day."

Take the filming of "I'm Not That Girl." It's just me on my own in a forest and all the film's elements are coming together. That's a big day.

Then "The Wizard and I." Elphaba starts at the bottom of the school and ends at the very top of a mountain. She literally ascends a peak and goes right up to the precipice. That is definitely not a small day.

And when Elphaba is talking about how her father hates her, and then she looks in the mirror and is told she's beautiful? That's a big moment.

In making *Wicked*, the hardest thing was to not look at everything we were hoping to do and just see it as a megalith, one overwhelming and massive task. We had to break it down into moments, bite-sized pieces, and find the charm in each. Even within each bite-sized frame, there were countless big moments that required a lot from us emotionally.

That's exactly how running a marathon is, as well as life. All the moments are important, adding to each other, accreting. We need to attend to each with our full selves and open hearts.

Taken one by one, these flashes of time add up to a life.

One of the aspects of Elphaba's character I loved as she's moving through her own series of big moments is that she's able to see past the veneer. She does it with Fiyero; she does it with Dr. Dillamond. She does it with the Wizard and even with Madame Morrible, though that one takes her a while. Initially, she feels accepted. Madame Morrible offers her the approval she's wanted her whole life.

I have been hated forever and now Madame Morrible thinks I have talent. My strange power, the very thing I thought was my destruction, she says is a gift!

That's heady stuff and it's no wonder she's unable to see Madame Morrible for who she is until it's almost too late.

Despite the pain of letting go of who she wants Madame Morrible to be for her, Elphaba has the courage to see her clearly. To pierce the thin veil between how Madame Morrible presents and who she really is.

It's likely Elphaba's able to do this because she's spent so long covering up her own pain, hiding what she's been going through, fortifying her own defenses. Sound familiar? When we are people who put up walls, we can see very clearly the walls of others. Our bullshit meter alerts us.

Like Elphaba, though, we can also learn to let go. When we see the obstacles others throw up to keep themselves safe, we can ask ourselves if we might be doing the same. *What pretense am I showing? What is this person unable to receive from me because I've put up defenses?*

Once we see it, we can drop it, which Elphaba learns to do.

Without those obstacles in the way, it's easier for people to receive from you who you really are and what you want to give.

Then we can enter each day knowing none of them are insignificant, able to see clearly. We can finally glimpse beyond the veneer to the remarkable fact of our own immense and anything-but-small lives.

143

38

You Do Not Need to Go to the Bathroom

I'm a pretty disciplined person and this quality has long served me well. But there are times knowing I can override my body—like when I'm running and I urge myself to go farther and faster than I want to—can be detrimental. I have to learn balance if I don't want to get hurt. I have had to learn to listen to my body, which is not always a simple task. For me, fairness to myself and moderation do not come easy.

While filming *Wicked*, though, I was really glad to know I could make up my mind about something physical and just expect my body to pull it off. There are times to call upon that authority and put it to work.

I'm thinking of all that was needed to make Elphaba come to life. The processes of doing her hair, makeup, and costume were arduous and time consuming. Even just taking off the green at the end of the day took an hour and a half; I was often the last person on set.

A lot of thought went into her makeup. For instance, none of what went on my face, except for shades to add definition, contouring, and texture, was any other color than green. The eyeliner was green; the eyeshadow, green. Lipstick, green. Lip liner, green. All shades of green, but we used different shades to find dimension. That was something I wanted. We even had a green gel so the palms of her hands were green but still looked like palms.

Once I was green, I'd dress in a costume made of layers. Green tights that matched my body makeup. On top of that, fishnet stockings, which I adored. Then a corset, pulled in, before the shirt, the dress, or whichever costume I was in that day. I was corseted all the time.

If I was to be flying on a given day, I'd also wear both a harness and a special costume fitted with pit points that allowed my harness to be connected to the wires. That harness needed to be snug to keep me safe.

But here's the thing. Once all this was on, it was a huge pain to get out of and then back into again. Wires and whatnot. So I would tell myself each morning, at seven or eight a.m., "Well, this is it for the next twelve or fourteen hours. I will not need to use the bathroom." This was probably a terrible idea, but it was what I needed to do. Throughout the day, people would ask if I needed the bathroom. But I wasn't going to do it. I was not playing.

And as it worked out, in fact, I did not need to use the bathroom on those days. But that doesn't make strong-arming myself on a regular basis a good thing.

I'm starting to learn that having a limit does not actually make you limited. In running marathons, performing, and other parts of life, my body can only do so much. When I run a lot, I need to take time off to rest. When I'm rested, I can run farther and faster the next time. The same was true when I was in a harness. I would need to take time away from flying on one day in order to heal. Then I would be able to do more flying the next day. When we put limits in place, they allow us to expand how much we can actually do.

I think for many of us, we see the opposite of determination as giving up, quitting, weakness. But it's not at all. It's true power. Paying attention to your body and its deep wisdom is judicious and smart.

Are you able to listen to your body? It's tough sometimes, but I'm trying.

If we want to be simply more in this life, it's good to have limits. Except when you're in an elaborate costume.

39

Do Not Let Rage Define You

I don't agree with the idea that we should bite back our anger and swallow our rage to make ourselves more acceptable to others. When we allow ourselves to be simply more, sometimes that means being more righteously angry. But the pendulum can swing too far and hurt us in the end.

That's like swallowing poison and hoping the person who wronged you will die.

Elphaba is angry, and she has reasons to be. She's actually throbbing with hurt and pain. She doesn't live in her rage 24/7, but it's literally on her skin, always at the surface. And she handles these sharp emotions differently from me. I had to figure out her rhythm; it's not the same as mine.

The truth, I came to see, is that she's not angry at the entire world all the time. Mostly, she accepts how she's viewed by others, and she makes peace with that fact. She doesn't hold it against anyone. It is what it is.

Because, really, if she were mad at the world the entire time, how would she function? She can hold her anger in one hand and her joy in the other. Both are parts of the whole. One does not eclipse the other.

Dealing with strong feelings like rage and learning to channel them in a productive way has taken me time. I don't think any of us is born knowing how to do this.

For a number of years, I went from one toxic manager to another. One in particular treated me as if I didn't know anything at all and seemed to feel I had no right to ask questions. Over time, that attitude grated on me, and then our conflict came to a head.

I was getting ready to do a live performance at the Greek Theatre in Los Angeles that was going to be used as promotional material for a series I'd done, and he mentioned at the last minute that he was bringing a bunch of people from "the office" to watch me rehearse and prepare.

"Who are they?" I asked.

He wouldn't say who.

"Why are they coming?"

Again, he wouldn't tell me and seemed to think my questions didn't deserve his attention.

Now, I'm very particular about who gets to be in my space. It's an energy exchange. I take in energy and I give out energy. The people I'm around just before I perform can have a huge impact on me. In fact, I usually want to be alone beforehand to focus myself or, if not alone, with people whose energy I know feels good and who will be supportive.

It was half an hour before I was going to perform when the manager sprang this on me. He didn't ask if they could come and talk with me. He simply told me I would meet these people because it was the gracious and grateful thing to do. I was already in makeup and no matter what questions I asked for clarification, he wouldn't give a straight answer. Why was he doing this? I was so confused. Feeling out of control is a symptom of past traumas and this was smack bang on top of a trigger. If he had an explanation that made sense, I would have understood. But he was evasive. And I was expected to be okay with it. There was the assumption that my space was not my own and that I should be grateful for the fact they were coming at all.

The rage exploded from me. It was bad. I was furious. I don't think I've had an outburst like that before or since. To be honest, I even scared myself. I utterly blacked out with rage.

Thankfully, I had friends there who diffused the situation and asked the manager to leave. He did. And that was the last time I saw him. But after, he sent me an email resigning as my manager and chastising me.

"Never in my sixteen-year career have I had an exchange with an artist like that," he wrote, calling my energy "dismissive, cold, irrational, weird, dark," and saying it "lacked kindness and gratitude." He said that he'd tried to explain what was happening, that he wanted me to meet these people who

149

had worked hard to make all this happen, and I had literally lashed out at him. He called what had happened a "temper tantrum," and said I owed him and everyone present an apology for my behavior. "It was hard to watch!" he admonished.

He went on to pinpoint what had really occurred. "I can assure you that you are holding on to some kind of trauma," he wrote.

He was not wrong, and though I'd tried to address it in the room—hence my request for clarification—he didn't listen but only exacerbated the trauma. As it turned out, I did in fact meet the people "from the office" after the show and did apologize to the others who had been present during my outburst. But by not addressing the conflict directly with me, he replicated exactly what my father had done years ago. He left, taking no responsibility for his role in the confrontation.

The suggestion that I was ungrateful really got to me. It implies that you are somehow lesser, that you need to take up less space.

Forget that. Forget him. If I can't have people in my space who get me, who can support me, I don't want them there at all.

I realized two things from that experience. One, that people will often blame you when you're simply standing your ground, and that if they do, they are not your people. It's best to move as far away from them as possible.

And two, I saw my past anger leaping into my present, coloring what was happening. I've heard it said that if it's hysterical, it's historical. My feelings were deepened and sharpened by my father's abandonment. And the all-too-often suggestion that asking "Why?" or saying "No" is a display of my inadequacy and not simply requests to have more information about what is happening to me. I'd never been able to ask my father, "Why?" He'd never supplied me with a clear reason he had hurt me in such a way. And so to have that manager not give me an answer to a very straight-forward question felt like that event occurring in the present moment.

I hope that occurrence between myself and my manager maybe taught him a lesson or two, though something tells me that's unlikely. I can only hope that whoever he managed after me was strong enough to keep asking why, or calm enough to not disappear into rage.

I've had many painful disappointments in my life and have always asked why. When the person answers that question with clarity and does not blame me or become defensive, I can accept what's happening. But the refusal to answer that question, to dishonor my need to understand, infuriates me. And especially when the person tries to blame me.

I have had to learn how to navigate those moments with-out blowing my top. How to establish and hold my boundar-ies without throwing a fit. How to hold my anger in one hand and honor and respect for myself in the other.

There needs to be room for both. There needs to be hope of moving forward.

Otherwise the rage and anger will consume everything.

I think of Celie in *The Color Purple*. She could spend all

her time allowing justifiable rage to shape her. Or she could decide she'd harness her own power and find happiness instead.

Many of us will always wrangle with these questions. When we're wronged, when we're outraged, how much grace do we give to others who have harmed us? How much of ourselves do we hold back? How do we learn to trust again? Should we trust again?

We can always choose to simply position ourselves out of reach of those who have hurt us, and then move on.

Rage can be powerful. But not if it defines you.

40

How Badly Do You Want It?

We had only twelve days left to complete the filming of both installments of *Wicked* when the writers' strike brought everything to a halt. We were so close to the finish line. I'd been ready for ages. Game fit. Good to go.

Still, I had to accept the fact it was unlikely we'd be coming back anytime soon.

I continued to keep my body ready, working out as if I were still on set, doing everything I could. Feeding myself well. Making sure I was strong and that my voice was the way I needed it to be. I was checking in regularly to see if anything in the negotiations had changed, but I also worked to let go so I didn't drive myself insane. There was only so much I could control and I needed to make peace with what I couldn't.

One hundred forty-eight excruciating days later, the call came. We were finally going back to work!

After all that standing by, I was chomping at the bit, eager to complete the job. I started rehearsals and training for flying immediately, ecstatic to be working again. But after only one day back, on the 8th of January, my birthday, I found myself utterly totaled.

I'd contracted the worst flu ever.

I was sick, sick, sick. You know the kind when the fever comes on, pummels you before breaking, and you think you're in the clear? But then it all comes roaring back again and you're wrecked even worse this go-around. It was a kind of sick that was downright concerning. My skin was hurting.

And all I could think was, *When is this going to stop?*

It went on and on. I was down for the count. So ill. And so annoyed with myself. Why was this happening now?

The universe was asking me, *Cynthia, how badly do you want it?* The universe was forcing me to earn it, really earn it.

Because once I got well and we finished the films, I knew in a bone-deep way that was so unbelievably satisfying that despite it all—the sickness, delays, chafing, falls, obstacles—I had done it. We'd done it together.

Everything else—what the world would say in response, how the films would be received—was almost beside the point.

The universe had asked me how badly I wanted it and

I had answered with a full-throated cry: *I want it with all that I am!*

What I learned is that when you think you have passed the final test, another one may be around the next corner. Mountaineers experience this all the time, reaching false summits before the final peak. Don't give up. Don't be surprised, just buckle down. You've got this.

41

Allow What You Can't Fathom

Wicked became a thing and Mattel wanted to make a Barbie with my face on it. Something shifted in me with that Barbie because I was able to take a little control over what she looked like.

I would like my eyes to not be so small.

I would like to not make my nose tiny.

I would like to keep my lips big and juicy.

Please and thank you.

What this meant was that a different form of beauty was now available for little girls to take home with them. A lot of the previous Black Barbies I'd seen had Eurocentric features paired with dark skin.

This one was different. While others were milestones, this

one gave me an opportunity to shift our features into the mainstream.

The features looked like mine, reflecting my African heritage, and like my little goddaughters, who all adore the doll. The daughter of my makeup artist Joanna was at my house the other day. Noelle, a sweetheart. And though she's a preteen and you'd think maybe too old for Barbies, she was telling her mother that she didn't have all the versions of me.

"I don't think I have the Sing Along one," she'd said pointedly.

There was something different about this Barbie. She was connecting to people who recognized her.

So now I was a Mattel Barbie. Hello?

My nose, my lips.

Me, who used to think I would never be cast as Elphaba because I was Black.

What was even happening?

In a similarly astonishing way, Ari and I could not have fathomed the response to the first installment of the film. I went through Times Square not too long ago and there was this ridiculously huge moving billboard with a poster of the both of us. I'd never seen myself that big in my life.

It was wild. The whole thing, wild.

But I think I did a better job this time than with *Harriet* or *The Color Purple*, being present with what was unfolding. Because we were going through it together.

The world premiere of the film was held in Australia, and we were all there. Jon and I had a number of special moments together, away from the crowds and the cameras, the awards and events. He's always been like a big brother to me. And we spoke from the heart.

"This is what I'm thinking," he said.

"This is what I'm feeling," I said.

And: "I love you."

"I love you too."

Though the film's staggering reception floored so many, it didn't fully surprise any of us. I think we all knew instinctively how special what we were making was. We all seemed to be very clear on that fact. And we all wanted to do not just a good job, but really take the most precious care of this material.

During filming, we zeroed in and got to work. But then, in the aftermath, we had to work on something new.

Allowing all this wonderfulness to be exactly what it was.

Allowing all we could not have possibly fathomed to exist.

Allowing it to be simply more than we'd expected.

Experiencing positive emotions can be hard for some of us. Sometimes, we're so used to pushing through obstacles and setbacks, being scrappy and proving ourselves, that we don't know how to respond when we finally reach our goal.

What are the experiences you may need to allow? Can you let go and just let them happen?

42

No One Has the Right to Say Shit

I've been a specimen in a petri dish since I was a teenager. I've heard it all, every version of what's wrong with me. And when I fix it, then it's wrong for different reasons.

Maybe you've felt the same?

Even just the simplest things like your appearance. It's hard to protect yourself from that noise. And it's uncomfortable no matter what scale you're experiencing it on.

If you go to Thanksgiving dinner and someone's granny says, *Oh, my God, you look skinnier, what's wrong?*

Or someone else says, *You look heavier, what happened?*

That is uncomfortable and horrible no matter where it's happening. Unfortunately, in today's society, there's a degree of ease involved in commenting on others. Their looks, what people think might be going on behind the scenes, their health, or how they present themselves. Whether they are strangers, family members, or even people you call friends, they feel they have a right to talk about everything,

from what you're wearing,

to your body

to your hair

to your face

This ease in making remarks is really dangerous for all parties involved.

I'm lucky to have the support system I have, and to trust that and know deep down that I'm beautiful—and so are you.

But I *do* know what the pressure of that noise feels like. It's been a resident in my life since I was seventeen. But now, I just don't invite it in anymore. It's not welcome. I have work to do. I have a life to live. I have friends to love on. I have so much love, and other people's negative energy is simply not well received. I don't leave space for it anymore.

We can protect ourselves from that noise, whether it's at a family reunion or online. You can block people; I don't care if you have to delete the app entirely. You can keep yourself safe because no one has the right to say shit.

43

Celebrate Yourself

I dress for me.

Clothing for me is a love language, and that includes everything from my piercings, to my nails, to what I put on my body, to my jewelry. Everything I wear speaks to me and who I am as a person. It represents the style I want to express and the story I want to tell.

Some people are more sedate with what they wear, and that works for them. But I'm just not. I've been this way for a really long time, though people seem to notice it a lot more now. I'm a happy rebel and I really am not concerned with whether people like it. By showing myself fully in this way, I hope I'm encouraging others to be themselves.

Sometimes we dress because we want people to compliment us, or we want to be on someone's best-dressed list. I dress the way I do because it gives me joy. I adore clothes. I love to dress up. I find jewelry irresistible; the idea of adorning oneself is a thing I subscribe to. I was collecting costume pieces when I was fifteen and sixteen. At the time, I was doing backing vocals and needed earrings, necklaces, bangles. Now, I have twenty-one piercings and I'm a geek about how my jewelry is made and who makes it. I'll seek out random boutiques and designers that nobody else in the world knows because I'm attracted to what they do.

It's just how I am.

People ask questions about my nails constantly. A question that stuck out to me was when I was asked if my nails were a kind of shield, keeping others at arm's distance, an observation I found kind of funny. I've been doing my nails since I was sixteen, though I stopped for a year or so because of a small role I was playing on Broadway . . . and that's usually the only reason I would stop. Far from being a shield, my nails actually bring people to me. Others are not afraid to come close to look at my fingers, to hold my hand and examine the work. People I invite in are unafraid to enter my personal space because of the nails, and I welcome that. Plus, the artists who make my nails possible are really special people and they use my fingers as their canvas. I love getting to show off their work.

Maybe it's not in your clothes, jewelry, or nails, but we

all need ways to show our deepest selves and invite others to connect with who we really are.

Whatever you do, be sure you celebrate the one-of-a-kind, exceptional human you are. Make that uniqueness visible.

44

Decide, and Let It Be So

Proving yourself over and over again? I've done it, and still do sometimes.

Let's let go of that nonsense this very minute.

Because no matter what you do, how hard you work, how much you accomplish, it's never enough. We have to leave grasping for recognition behind and understand we're never going to prove to some that we are enough.

We have to find a way to prove ourselves simply to ourselves.

That is huge.

You can't prove yourself to anyone else; it doesn't work. You will constantly be chasing their approval and you won't even know exactly what they want or what they are waiting for you to do—or even if they're waiting for a damned thing.

So prove yourself to yourself.

Today.

Decide that you are enough.

Decide, and let it be so.

And as you wonder if the things you're desiring will ever come your way, remember that whatever is for you will find you. If it does not, it was not supposed to come in the first place.

Either way, we are good enough. We are doing the work to prepare ourselves for what might be coming. We are becoming authentically ourselves.

And that, dear ones, is our primary job, the work of this lifetime.

45

Assemble Your Team

I like to have "no" people around me.

Of course, it's important to have people who encourage us and tell us we can do whatever we set our minds to, but it's equally important to have those who are willing to question what we're doing and who can reflect back to us what they see. They can help us see beyond ourselves. For that reason, I try to surround myself with people who have more experience than I do, people who know more. I do not ever want to be the cleverest person in the room because if I'm that person, I'm not learning. Being teachable allows me to not betray myself, to remain in a position of openness and curiosity. Knowing less means my mission is consistently to learn and grow.

When I recorded my first album, it was during the pandemic and we were doing it over Zoom, which was not ideal. I was trying to put something together that had to come from the very core of me and it wasn't working. It took a while to realize why.

I was working with so many people who each had their own agenda and their own idea of what I should be doing. We were clashing and I didn't know what to do about it.

More recently, I've recorded a new album and it's been an altogether different and remarkably better experience. And that's because to do so, I first assembled my team and made sure it was composed of people who held the same vision I did, but who would also push back on me and tell me no if that's what was needed to reach our shared goal.

The truth is, I expect a lot from people. And I don't really mince my words with anyone. You get straight shooting from me, immediately, which isn't always easy to be around. Plus, I ask all the time, "What are we doing here?" and "Why?"

This new experience, creating this album, presented me with the chance to build and discover a team who were willing to see the creative vision I saw for myself. I was introduced to my new artists and repertoire (A&R) person, Wendy Goldstein, who develops musical talent at the record label. Wendy's magic comes from consistently thinking about the why. So often, she could answer the why without me requesting it. I'm not even sure she was consciously doing so. Either way, we were definitely a match.

And my manager Jess, who willingly took on the responsibility of managing me as a musician, which requires a totally different skill set. I trust her because she ALWAYS answers my whys but lovingly challenges me when we disagree.

Part of the magic of Wendy and Jess and many others on my team is that they actually answer the question I keep asking ad nauseam. "Why?" Everyone on my team, likewise, is open and honest. Everyone is forthcoming, which makes for a very different experience.

I think back to twelve-year-old Cynthia who was told she was too much, too nosy, and asking too many questions. Always "Why?" But once I surrounded myself with people who respected me enough to answer that question truthfully, everything was good.

This is a wonderful metaphor for life. People who have the willingness to answer that question are generally secure in themselves and they don't fear exposure; that's who you want by your side.

To be honest, I think sometimes I test people with that question. Maybe unknowingly, I ask to see just how honest a person will be. Say I ask someone to do something and they say no. If I ask why and they answer with, "I just don't have it in me," I'm good. That answer satisfies me because it comes from an honest place, even if I wish they'd said yes. I understand. If my previous manager had said to me, when I asked why, that he actually didn't know how to manage my project, I would have known what to do next. "Thank you for saying that. Thank you for giving me the opportunity to decide whether to move forward or to make another choice."

When you're surrounded by people who tell you the truth, the power is in your own hands. You get to make the decision on which way you're going to go. You're not a victim of someone else's choices and what they think. I need to be able to make my own choices in this life. And what helps me with that is information, answers to things I am unsure of.

We all need that.

Assemble your team. Don't do this life alone. Just make sure those around you are willing to tell you the truth, even when it's not what you want to hear. They are the people you need.

And whatever you do, be sure to let them know how much you appreciate them. Be sure to say thank you.

46

Keep Breathing

I just don't abide by the idea you can only have so much in life. Why? If I work hard enough and I know what I want, I can have what I desire. And when I do it from a pure heart, when I do it with hard work, when I do it because I enjoy doing it, some of that can be siphoned off for someone else.

The more that comes my way, the more I can give. If I limit the amount I can fill myself with, then I limit the amount I can give away as well—to worthy causes, to people asking me for advice, to friends who need me. If I'm not filling myself with the things I love and I am not going after the aspirations I harbor, if I'm not seeking, striving, reaching for the things I desire, then I stop aspiring altogether.

as·pire

/əˈspī(ə)r/

aspired; aspiring

intransitive verb

1: to seek to attain or accomplish a particular goal

2: ascend; soar

Etymology

Middle English, from Middle French or Latin; Middle
French *aspirer*, from Latin *aspirare*, literally, to breathe
upon, from *ad-* + *spirare* to breathe[*]

I'd rather keep reaching upward than standing in one
space and not moving. I'd rather keep breathing. Striving
for more is as natural as breathing, and don't let anyone tell
you otherwise.

---

[*] "aspire." *Merriam-Webster Dictionary*, 2025. merriam-webster.com/
dictionary.

47

My Happiness Is for Me First

My energy, my life force
It is for me, first
When I am well resourced
I have much to share
But my happiness is mine first
It's why I don't talk about
My relationships
I spend so much of my life
Sharing
everything—
My work, my soul, my voice, my words, my art.
I give of myself willingly
I'm choosing to keep something
for me

Maybe I'll change my mind at some point
Things you know:
I'm queer
A person who loves
And is loved
Who can have, who will have, who has had
Relationships
with men or women or neither
It's enough for people to know I am loved
And I am happy.
Besides what is life
Without a little

Mystery?

48

Find Daily Joys

We're so programmed to look for the big wins that it is sometimes hard to see the daily joys before us. I have to remind myself all the time to seek out and notice those easily overlooked moments of delight that make up my day.

If I don't look, I'm likely to miss them.

Recently, I needed to go see my trainer and decided that instead of getting a car, I'd take my Razor scooter, the kind you see kids riding. No motor, just (wo)man power. What I didn't realize when I set out was that it was almost all uphill, and motorless Razor scooters don't work so well uphill. Nonetheless, I persevered. I listened to music, I encouraged myself, I laughed along the way. And when I made it there in one piece, despite the silliness of this literal uphill journey, I was so proud of myself. Giddy little moments like that bring me such enjoyment, but I have to stay on the lookout for them.

I recently planned a party for my mother's seventieth birthday. It wasn't a big project, but doing it reconnected me with her, made me see how vibrant and special she is in my life, and reignited my deep love for her. Not that that flame ever went out, but sometimes we get busy; we don't see how important people are to us. And doing this party—making choices of food and venue, and coming up with sweet little details that tickled her—tenderized my heart, made me see again how very much I love her.

These small enjoyments are vital.

Another place I find daily bliss is in the sauna. Each morning when my schedule allows, I'm in there for an hour. It looks as if I'm simply caring for my body, but it's more than that.

Because my sauna door is glass, I can see outside. The garden fills with all kinds of different birds. Recently a hummingbird has been showing up, dancing for me on the other side of the glass. So now, whenever I take a sauna, it's with the secret hope that the hummingbird will come back again. What does that flitty little creature have to gain by dancing before me—isn't that just a waste of its energy? But no, the hummingbird dances as it flies, as it adds to my day, expressing its joy with everything it does.

Hummingbirds are my favorite. I remember hearing the tale of a hummingbird during a forest fire; I think it might be a Native American story. When the fire hit, all the animals fled before it until they came to a stream and found safety there. They were frozen in fear because their home, the forest, was being taken from them. No matter how big or strong they were, they were all paralyzed by the fear of what was happening.

Except for the hummingbird. It flitted down to the stream, dipped its little beak in the water, and pulled up one droplet, all the hummingbird could hold. It then flew back to the fire despite its fear and dripped its one tiny droplet onto the fire. Again and again it flew back and forth, one droplet at a time. The other forest animals discouraged the hummingbird, told it that it was too small to make a difference, that its efforts were wasted. The hummingbird was undeterred, determined to do whatever it could to help.

And that's all any of us can do, isn't it? In the face of all the world's injustices, we do our own little bit. Watching that brilliantly colored flying jewel of a creature out the sauna window, dancing for no reason other than the sheer elation of movement, reminds me of who I am and what I'm trying to do in life.

This is why we look for joy.

There was a time when I struggled to name my daily joys, when I failed to notice them. But once I made a commitment to myself to discover them and looked deeper, my whole being changed. Those of us who are focused and driven can sometimes miss these small pleasures.

But trust me, you don't want to miss them.

49

Move Past What You No Longer Need

After my father abandoned me when I was sixteen, I desperately wanted to show him I was extraordinary—so he would love me. It's as simple and as complicated as that.

But I no longer look to him for love. And you don't need to look to those who don't see you for who you are either.

I release my father from his paternal role. I harbor no animosity toward him. Today, I am completely neutral about him.

I have come to understand he was never meant to be a dad. I think he was meant to be the person who got me on Earth and was then meant to go on with his own life as a separate human being.

We assume our parents are *only* our parents simply because we're their kids. I read in a book by a wise human being that we fail to see that before our parents were parents, they were human beings with lives of their own. Maybe some of these humans are only meant to bring children into the world, not necessarily raise them.

The truth is, if my dad were to have raised me, I'd have no idea where I would be today.

And yes, I spent a long time working to make him see how worthy I was of his love. But I've since come to learn that I am completely worthy regardless of what he thinks. And in truth, I do my creative work for me.

Today, I'm really enjoying this life for myself. Wherever he is, I want him to know that I'm okay with the fact we don't have a relationship. Because in truth, we don't need it.

I'm not asking him for a relationship.

I absolve him. And I am free.

50

Believe in Something

As we go through life and lean into being simply more, it's important to believe in something bigger than ourselves. For me, that something is God. But it can be whatever you regard as indisputably good and life-affirming: community, love, family, nature. The important thing is to acknowledge we're not the center of the universe. We're one among countless unique creations, all imbued with our creator's vision. The Bible tells us we're all made in God's image. Not just some people, not just those we personally approve of or agree with.

All of us.

I was raised Roman Catholic, but over time that faith tradition began to feel restrictive and too rules based. Formal religion works for many and I appreciate and honor that fact. But for me, when I focused on all the rules, I lost track of what I now believe to be the most important parts of my own creed, of what I believe faith—at least my own—is supposed to be. In order to create space inside myself to form my own understanding of what I believed and why I believed it, I had to let go of the formal aspects of religion.

Right now, I'm really clear that the most important part of my faith is to be loving and kind to people and the world, to deeply honor the wonder and life that surrounds and blesses me. No one is more special or holy or worthy than anyone else. Sparks of God reside in all of us.

And the kindness I offer is not limited to people. I have two dogs, so I care for them in the most tender way possible because I want that loving-kindness to come back to me. I believe things are cyclical. If you give out something good, something good will come back. You might not see it immediately, but somehow it finds its way back like a boomerang. That is the most important part of my faith. To offer goodness and kindness whenever possible, and to appreciate as deeply as I can all that comes to me.

I say "thank you" a lot. Those two words on their own are a complete prayer.

And this is why the criticism I've received for taking on the role in *Jesus Christ Superstar* is, to me, incredible and painful. By playing that role, I hope to remind people that we are all meant to live up to the ideals Jesus championed. And part of that is to be fully ourselves because that's where our creator's vision is most keenly visible.

Alas, not everyone agrees.

I just received an email from a woman I've never met, outraged by my choice.

"Having a woman play Jesus is grossly inappropriate and is a mockery of our beloved Savior . . . this is incredibly disrespectful and blasphemous," she wrote. "I urge you to . . . cancel your participation in this production."

Sadly she sees me, another woman, as inappropriate and blasphemous for playing this role. So often in life, we are chastised for doing what other people see as wrong—for stepping out farther than they would do themselves, for being simply more than they want for their own lives.

But just because they see it that way does not mean it is not ours to do.

Being more, even a little more than other people are comfortable with, is seldom easy. Sometimes you're told you're unreasonable or excessively demanding, that you're exorbitant or immoderate. But if we're going to live up to our full humanity and become our complete and unabridged selves, allowing ourselves to be the most we can be is absolutely necessary.

In this case, I believe this woman is really talking about what she thinks of herself as a woman. And that is simply heartbreaking.

Women are sacred, powerful beings, and the reason most nations try to control what we do, who we marry, how we have sex, who we have sex with, how we dress, what we cover and don't cover is because if they were to stop doing that, women around the globe might realize just how powerful we

are. That scares a lot of people, including some women themselves who then take on the role of policing us, their sisters,
other women, not realizing their own lives don't become
better by doing so.

The saddest thing for me about this email is that the writer
doesn't realize she is talking about herself—which is devas-
tating. For a woman to send this to another woman is to say
she sees herself as a lesser being than a man.

I don't believe that of myself. Nor of other women. Nor
of any other human.

None of us are lesser beings.

I was struck by her reaction, and yet she's not the only
person. Many imply that I should not take on the role since I
am a Black, queer woman. I am someone outside the mainstream. I am not what they expect. I am asking for or taking
too much.

What these critics are really saying is that I don't *deserve*
to play this role. Over the years, the role of Jesus has been
played by many different people and never generated this
kind of controversy. Are these critics suggesting that Black,
queer women cannot also be spiritual beings? Cannot play
roles imbued with spirituality?

I come back again to the fact the Bible says that each person is made in the likeness of God. That includes me. And
you. And everyone else.

51

When You're Attacked

Some say that once you stop being the underdog, you become the target. As we journey along, becoming simply more, the question then becomes how we can anchor ourselves in those tough moments.

There's no question it's difficult because you're human and that shit hurts. You can't pull everyone aside and say, *Now wait a minute, that's not true. Here's who I actually am. Please see me for who I really am.*

You can't do that with everybody. All you can do is consistently show up with your best self—that doesn't mean your perfect self. That's simply too hard and we'll end up failing because everything is always perfectly imperfect. Just our best self, with the best of intentions. Every single time.

And keep doing the work.

Keep showing up in a way that asserts your humanity. Understand that the people who attack you don't actually know you, and you don't know them. You don't know what they're going through and they don't know what you're experiencing. That's okay.

Maybe one day they'll reassess. They might come back and say, *Actually she's not so bad after all.*

But that is not yours to fix or solve. Yours is to make sure the people who have made the effort to get to know you really do know you. That they are given the opportunity to see you deeply.

And when people attack, don't shut down. Don't shrink. There are others in the world who may be looking to you, at you, who may be using you as their inspiration.

Do not let the attackers win. Show your beautiful self in all your glory.

52

For Those Who Are Out and Proud, and Those Still Waiting

Toni Morrison once said, "The function of freedom is to free someone else." I think about that a lot.

My life and career have been a wild, wild ride and I'm grateful for every second. But more than anything, I appreciate how open-armed my queer community has been.

I have spoken about being your whole self, your true self. I speak about the prizes that come from being *you* against the odds. But rarely do I acknowledge how hard that can be.

I want to make room for those of us who are trying to find the courage to exist as we want.

It isn't easy. None of it is. Waking up and choosing to be yourself. Proclaiming a space belongs to you when you don't feel welcomed. Teaching people on a daily basis how to address you. The frustrations of re-teaching people words that have been in the human vocabulary since the dawn of time.

They. Them.

Words used pedantically to describe two or more people. Poetically, to describe a person who is simply *more*.

It isn't easy to ask people to treat you with dignity; it should be a given. It isn't easy to learn to grow into who you are when the world around you is knocking at your door, telling you to stay inside.

Some flowers, like the peony, bloom against all the odds. But most need to be tended and cared for before they brave the light and open their petals to the sun.

186

For those of us who consider ourselves "out and proud," know we have all been recipients of a great gift, the opportunity to be *more*. For many, the road to that place was not paved with yellow bricks but bumps and potholes. Whatever road you have traveled, how beautiful it is that you had a road to travel at all.

Remember, there are the invisible ones who have no road, who have not even yet begun to find their road.

If you are that person who has not yet found your road, be encouraging and patient with yourself. The way forward will show itself. You might not have had the strength or capacity to fully become yourself just yet. That's okay. Know that I am proud of your quiet and solitary *want* to be fully yourself.

And for the rest of us, know that our real work is to make the ground we leave in our wake level enough for the person who is searching for their road and has not found it yet. We are called to be lanterns for each other. On your journey to showing the world who you are, light up the path for others.

Some of us can afford to be seen. We see each other. I see you. You see me.

But think of those who have not yet been seen, those who sit in the dark and wait their turn, hoping for a spark to light their way.

I ask every single one of you, in the spaces you're in and with the lights you hold. Point illumination in the direction of someone who needs a little guidance.

Be that lantern.

Pronouns

She
Her
Hers
Me

Just shining some light.

Good Night and God Bless

Every night, it's like clockwork. I pick out the pajamas I'm going to wear to bed. What I select will depend on the weather and how I want to feel. All my pajamas are matched sets in varying colors and/or patterns. I like pima cotton or silk. Touches of lace can be exquisite. And this may sound absurd, but sometimes I pick a waffle cashmere set with a hoodie and loose, cropped, wide trousers. I get cold at night.

Each outfit has its matching robe, either a big, warm, flowy duster cardigan or an actual robe; I like walking around feeling something close to me. I pull out my slippers, fluffy on the inside and closed-toed to keep my feet warm.

Nighttime is simply another excuse to dress up. My pajamas are outfits; putting them on feels like a way of honoring myself and the work I've done that day. I like to dress for bed.

Often, no one else sees me in these outfits, just me. But that's the whole point. They're meant for me, to please me.

Next, I make some kind of nighttime tea. I always have a huge mug of tea with me. Then I'll get cozy, maybe put on a movie or a TV show for a bit, and then I'll journal to reconnect with my innermost self. This is a chance to make sure I'm being loyal to myself and deeply loving to myself.

Then finally, sleep. Dream time. A chance to rest. Sleep restores me, allows me to get up and do it all over again.

As you go to bed tonight, assess where and how deeply you're caring for yourself. Honor yourself with a ritual, whether time-tested or brand new.

Being simply more is not easy work. We are called to be our most authentic and true selves hour after hour, day after day. And while it's the most rewarding way to live, it can also take a toll. So we need to remember to be good to ourselves.

Let's review the day.

We ran a good race. We gave it our all. And we will get a whole new chance to have a go at it again tomorrow.

Well done. These are the moments that make up a life, and when we choose them consciously, we build the lives we want.

Sleep well, dear friend. Your rest is hard won.

Good night and God bless.

Acknowledgments

On any creative journey there are and always will be moments that call for solitude, but inevitably that will not sustain; support is needed. Encouragement is needed. Guidance is needed. This book is no different. My name is on the cover, yes, but I did not do this alone, so permit me then to share at least some of the names of those who have made this possible.

My wonderful manager, Jessica Morgulis, who understands me and believes in everything I choose to put my mind to. She keeps me on track and extends amazing patience to me, making sure I'm always moving forward with my vision without ever rushing me. I am so grateful for your love and support.

My literary agent, Albert Lee, and all at UTA who carried me forward on this excursion of truth telling, and who told me from the beginning, and constantly, that I had something important to say.

Luvvie Ajayi Jones, whose advice has been invaluable. Thank you, big sister!

My publicists, the ladies at Lede—Meredith O'Sullivan, Michelle Margolis, and Samantha Cooper—who help position me to be seen in the light of my truest self.

Dr. Tom, my therapist, who has been instrumental in helping me discover the corners of myself that I may have been too afraid to mine on my own; without the knowledge of those parts, this book could not have been written. I owe him an endless debt of gratitude.

To Norman Jean Roy, who took the photo on this front cover and his exquisite wife, Jojo, who have constantly showed me kindness and have opened up their home to me both when I needed to nurse a broken heart and then when I needed to nurse a broken body after an actual marathon.

Thank you to everyone at Flatiron Books, including editor extraordinaire and publisher Megan Lynch, the wonderful editorial assistant Kara McAndrew, our amazing copy editor Michelle Li, and many more. Laywan Kwan and Kelly Gatesman on the Flatiron art team drew inspiration from the collage work of Miss Lorna Simpson, whose works we all adore, to turn a photograph I was proud of into a cover that I am equally proud of. You all made this such an amazing, heart-affirming experience.

And Bernadette Murphy, who has painstakingly and patiently helped me to craft the things I wanted to say. She listened and helped me get to the heart of the message I wanted to share. Thank you for being the best guide anyone could wish for as I shaped the raw material of my experiences into this narrative.

Thank you all for your love and service.

About the Author

Cynthia Erivo is a Grammy, Emmy and Tony Award-winning actress, singer, author and producer, as well as a SAG, Golden Globe and three-time Academy Award nominee. Since bursting onto West End and Broadway stages in *The Color Purple*, she has taken the world by storm. Erivo stars as Elphaba opposite Ariana Grande-Butera's Glinda in Universal's record-breaking film adaptation of the hit musical *Wicked* from director Jon M. Chu. *Wicked* opened at number one and has since become the highest-grossing movie based on a Broadway musical at the US box office. Erivo has received widespread critical acclaim for the role, which earned her Golden Globe, SAG, Critics' Choice, NAACP, BAFTA and Academy Award nominations.